D1627330

752
~~753~~

WORKING MEN'S COLLEGE

LIBRARY REGULATIONS.

The Library is open every week-day evening (except Saturday), from 6.30 to 10 o'clock.

This book may be kept for three weeks. If not returned within that period, the borrower will be liable to a fine of one penny per week.

If lost or damaged, the borrower will be required to make good such loss or damage.

Only one book may be borrowed at a time.

27757

TREASURY CONTROL

WORKING MEN'S COLLEGE
★ LIBRARY ★

TREASURY CONTROL

THE CO-ORDINATION OF
FINANCIAL AND ECONOMIC POLICY
IN GREAT BRITAIN

BY

SAMUEL H. BEER
PROFESSOR OF GOVERNMENT
HARVARD UNIVERSITY

WORKING MEN'S COLLEGE LIBRARY

OXFORD
AT THE CLARENDON PRESS
1956

Oxford University Press, Amen House, London E.C.4

GLASGOW NEW YORK TORONTO MELBOURNE WELLINGTON
BOMBAY CALCUTTA MADRAS KARACHI CAPE TOWN IBADAN

Geoffrey Cumberlege, Publisher to the University

WORKING MEN'S COLLEGE
LIBRARY

PRINTED IN GREAT BRITAIN
AT THE UNIVERSITY PRESS, OXFORD
BY CHARLES BATEY, PRINTER TO THE UNIVERSITY

PREFACE

THIS book is not concerned with all aspects of the Treasury's work, but only with its role as co-ordinator of financial and economic policy. This means that much of what the Treasury does has been almost entirely passed over, particularly the business of Establishments, Home Finance, and Overseas Finance. Yet if in this respect the theme of the book is narrow, in another it is as broad as the constitution itself. To try to understand the relations of the Treasury with the other great departments of state is to be led into an inquiry which ramifies throughout the complex and ancient architecture of British government. Fully to explain some simple Treasury decision—the result, let us say, of a telephone conversation between two Principals, one in the Treasury and the other outside; to try to find out why some things were said in this exchange and others were not and what has made possible the settlement which these two people have reached, would be a hardly less formidable undertaking than that on which Sir James Frazer embarked when he set out to understand the strange ceremony of the priests of Nemi.

Needless to say my inquiry has been less ambitious. But I have at least pushed it far enough to learn one lesson bearing on the interdependence of the various parts of British government. This is that with regard either to the Treasury alone or the government as a whole, it is impossible to describe what goes on at the official level without also considering events on the ministerial level. The responsibility of ministers for all official acts of their subordinates is a central convention of the constitution. In some sense, no doubt, this convention is a fiction; that is, many of the acts of his subordinates for which a minister is answerable to Parliament are not acts which he directly ordered or of which he would in the normal course even have knowledge. Critics sometimes push the point farther, suggesting, for instance, that Parliament demands so much of a minister's time and government has become so big and complicated that today the major decisions really are made by civil servants.

Ministerial responsibility would be a deep-dyed fiction indeed, if this were so. That it is not so is one conclusion of this book. We can hardly suppose that men who have fought their way to ministerial power will upon achieving it be content to surrender its exercise to subordinates. On the other hand, we need not imagine that men of the ability of the members of the Administrative Class are mere clerks, occupied solely with dotting the i's and crossing the t's of the orders of their political chiefs. They are appointed because they have judgement—and they use it. The official will advise his minister frankly and vigorously; once he has a ministerial decision, he will act boldly. But the official—in Britain at any rate—

profoundly needs that decision before he can act and it is highly unlikely that a department will be effective if its minister does not know his own mind. When the machinery of co-ordination at the official level runs smoothly, this is in no small degree owing to the fact that ministers do know their own minds and officials can therefore faithfully anticipate the decisions which their chiefs would or will make. Likewise, when ministers cannot agree—as, for instance, in the dying days of a coalition government—civil servants also will probably be unable to 'get on with the job'. Even with regard to matters which it does not directly discuss, therefore, the role of the Cabinet in co-ordination is critically important. Upon its drive and its harmony the success of official machinery very substantially depends. In this sense, ministerial responsibility, individual and collective, is no fiction but plain, unvarnished truth about what goes on in British government and administration.

Since printed sources on the work of the Treasury leave many aspects untouched, I have had to rely for information mainly on conversation with informed people. Most of them, being civil servants, must remain anonymous. These, as well as the members of parliament, journalists, and scholars who have talked to me about the Treasury, I wish to thank for their generous and indispensable help. I must, however, make it clear that, as regards both the selection of material and the interpretation placed upon it, the responsibility for this work is, of course, entirely my own.

I wish also to express thanks to the Social Science Research Council and to the Harvard Foundation for Advanced Research for grants which made it possible for me to get to Britain one summer for research on this book.

SAMUEL H. BEER

Harvard University

CONTENTS

very little additional employment and no permanent additional employment can, in fact, and as a general rule, be created by State borrowing and State expenditure'.[1] Whatever Government may come to power in the recognizable future, its and the Treasury's view is certain to touch wider horizons than those bounded by that doctrine.

The purposes of Treasury control have undergone a cautious, but emphatic, revolution. So also have the instruments through which it is exercised, the machinery of government at both the ministerial and official level having been very considerably altered. Yet the relationship of the Treasury and the 'great departments of state' bears a striking similarity to what it was in the past. The framing and co-ordination of economic policy and the processes of central economic planning have adapted themselves to the old model of Treasury control. The Treasury, as its officials themselves will say, is 'the traditional co-ordinating department', and its mode—one is tempted to say its 'style'—of co-ordination is derived from the past. New machinery has been erected and a new viewpoint guides Treasury control, but that term, commonly applied to the role of the 'liberal' Treasury, may still be applied to the role of the Treasury of the welfare state.

What is Treasury control? Any work on British government will lay stress on the importance and power

[1] 227 H.C. Deb. 54 (15 Apr. 1929).

of the Treasury. But what precisely does the Treasury do? And how does it do it? How is co-ordination achieved under Britain's peculiar plural executive? Given the large powers of the Treasury, should it not be said to direct and command rather than merely to co-ordinate? Where is the similarity between the old processes of Treasury control shaped by the Supply divisions and the new processes of economic planning? And how, incidentally, does the budgetary process over which the Treasury presides compare with that of the American system with its unitary executive?

The Treasury has not yet found its historian, nor have its present-day operations been subjected to close scrutiny by outside observers. Although the parliamentary side of British financial procedure has been fully described in many works, only one book on the Treasury as a whole has been published—Sir Thomas Heath's volume of 1927—and rare are the articles or special studies concerned with its operations within the administration.[1] At the outset, therefore, it will be necessary to give an account of the main parts of the Treasury—bare and brief, but serving at least the purposes of what the Army calls 'nomenclature'. Then we may turn to a description of the control exercised by the Supply divisions, comparing it afterwards with that of the new economic units of the Treasury. The concluding pages will be concerned with bringing out the factors in the

[1] See Note on Sources, p. 131.

3

British Civil Service and constitution which give co-ordination in British administration its peculiar style.

Since the time of Queen Anne the office of Lord High Treasurer has been in commission and formal control of the Treasury has been vested in a board of 'Lords Commissioners of Her (or His) Majesty's Treasury'. The board includes the First Lord of the Treasury, a post nowadays always held by the Prime Minister, the Second Lord of the Treasury, who is Chancellor of the Exchequer, and not more than five Junior Lords. The Junior Lords are Government Whips, serving under the Chief Whip, who has the title of Parliamentary Secretary of the Treasury. They play no part in the administration of the Treasury, except to sign certain formal documents from time to time. The Prime Minister's connexion with the Treasury is not purely nominal—he will, for instance, consult directly with the Permanent Secretary on questions of promotion to the highest positions in the Civil Service—but the minister in charge of, and responsible for, the department is the Chancellor of the Exchequer. He is assisted by two ministers, neither of whom is a member of the Treasury Board, the Financial Secretary to the Treasury and a minister of recent creation in charge of economic matters, the Economic Secretary.

Subject to such ministerial control, the Permanent Secretary stands at the head of the administrative hierarchy of the department. His salary is rather larger than that of other Permanent Secretaries and by long usage and by formal designation dating from 1919, he also enjoys the title of 'Official Head of the Civil Service'.[1] It is in this capacity that he advises the Prime Minister with regard to certain senior appointments in the Civil Service. In comparison with other departments the organization which he heads is small. In 1914 its personnel numbered 140, of whom 35 belonged to the Administrative Class. There was some growth between the wars and an enormous expansion in very recent years. Now the total is around 1,500 of whom some 200 belong to the Administrative Class. Among those, however, whom Dale would put in the 'higher civil service',[2] numbers are not so great as to prevent officials from seeing one another frequently and getting to know one another quite well.

Under the Permanent Secretary, who is assisted by a

[1] Since it is sometimes said that there is no formal document affirming this title of the Permanent Secretary it may be useful to quote the words of a Treasury Minute of 1919, repeated in a Treasury Circular of the same year. Referring to the Permanent Secretary, the minute says, 'He will act as permanent Head of the Civil Service and advise the First Lord in regard to Civil Service appointments and decorations.' (Quoted in Greaves, *Civil Service in the Changing State,* p. 177.) The expression 'Official Head of the Civil Service' makes sure that his office will be clearly distinguished from that of the supreme head of all the Services of the Crown, who is, of course, the Sovereign, and from that of the ministerial head of Her Majesty's Civil Service, who is the Prime Minister. For a controversial discussion of this question, see 125 H.L. Deb. 224 ff. and 275 ff. (25 and 26 Nov. 1942).

[2] See H. E. Dale, *The Higher Civil Service of Great Britain* (London, 1941).

deputy for economic and financial policy with the rank of Second Secretary, Treasury business is divided among five sides. (The term 'sides' is as close to a term of art to describe these parts of the Treasury as British usage comes; the term 'division' refers to a subordinate unit.) They are Establishments, Supply, Home Finance, Overseas Finance, and Economic Affairs. With Supply and Economic Affairs we shall deal at length later on. The work of Supply, which consists of the control of expenditure, including review of estimates, is conducted by seven divisions, each headed by an Under Secretary or Assistant Secretary and dealing with a group of departments administering similar or closely allied services.[1] Economic Affairs assists in the co-ordinaton of economic policy and planning, and its machinery includes the Central Economic Planning Staff and the Economic Section. In 1953 the CEPS, which had been in the charge of a Chief Planning Officer, was put under the newly created post of Deputy to the Permanent Secretary, and the Economic Section, which had long been virtually part of the Treasury, was formally transferred to the Treasury from the Cabinet Office, its head being given the title of Economic Adviser to Her Majesty's Government. Economic Affairs also includes a public relations unit, the Economic Information Division, which prepares briefs for ministers' speeches and press conferences, as well as news releases for press and radio,

[1] See organization chart at end.

and which assists the Central Office of Information in publicity campaigns.

Home and Overseas Finance deal respectively with the finance of government expenditure, including monetary policy, and with economic and financial relations with other countries. The Home Finance (Exchequer) Division handles the technical and executive work connected with the preparation of the Budget and the Finance Bill, although the precise size of the Budget and the proposed changes in taxation are dealt with at a high level in great secrecy until they are announced in the House of Commons. This division handles government relations with the Banks of England and Ireland and the National Debt Office, through which the public debt is managed, and maintains close liaison with the Board of Inland Revenue and the Board of Customs and Excise.

Home Finance (Capital) has the duty of advising on the most appropriate method of financing in line with the Government's general economic and financial policy. Among its duties is that of keeping in close contact with the Public Works Loan Board, the Development Areas Committee, and the Capital Issues Committee. The first two bodies are concerned with loans to local authorities and loans to companies wishing to conduct business in the development areas. To the Capital Issues Committee, which receives its policy instructions from the Chancellor of the Exchequer, come all applications for permission to make capital issues of £50,000 or over.

WORKING MEN'S COLLEGE LIBRARY

Closely connected with these two divisions are the two Treasury Officers of Accounts and the Treasury Accountant. The former, under the authority conferred on the Treasury by the Exchequer and Audit Act of 1866, control the form in which departments shall keep their accounts, a power which involves control over the form of departmental estimates. Under the same authority a Treasury Officer of Accounts also represents the Treasury at the hearings of the Public Accounts Committee of the House of Commons.

The Treasury Accountant has charge of payments from the Treasury's own vote and for certain other votes for which the Treasury is responsible. He is also responsible for issues to meet not only the service of the National Debt—whose detailed management is in the hands of the Bank of England—and other Consolidated Fund Services, but also the needs of the spending departments for funds. Controlling the formal disbursements to the Paymaster General, on whom departments directly draw, he is in a key position to watch over and to govern with some element of discretionary power the daily outflow of cash from the Central Government.

As Britain's international economic problems have become more critical, government control in this sphere has been extended and tightened and the business and size of the Overseas Finance side have grown accordingly. From the time of its separate establishment during the First World War and into the middle thirties, the work of this side of the Treasury was done by a single division. Today it includes ten divisions. Some are organized on a territorial basis and conduct the work of Overseas Finance as it relates to particular countries. Others are functional, dealing with the same problems— above all, of course, the problem of the balance of payments—but from the angle of special subjects, such as import programmes, exports, exchange control, American aid and relations with international bodies. With the important part played by Overseas Finance in co-ordinating interdepartmentally the import requirements of the economy as a whole, we shall be concerned in some detail later on.

Since we shall not deal with Establishments in the main body of this book, it may be given more attention at this point than the other sides of the Treasury. Much of its work, like that of Supply, consists in the control of other departments, being in fact one part of the former business of Supply which, because of its size and special character, was separated off and put into another set of divisions. And in the strictness of the control exercised by Establishments there has been a certain relaxation in recent years comparable to a similar change in control by the Supply divisions proper.

In the prevailing British view, control over expenditure necessarily involves control over establishments. With few exceptions officials and independent students alike reject the suggestion that a commission or other body outside the Treasury be given authority over the conditions of government employment. The scope of the British Civil Service Commission, therefore, is severely limited in comparison with that of the American, being confined principally to questions relating to entry into the service. The principal duties of the Establishments divisions are to control the numbers and grades employed in departments and to control conditions of service throughout the Civil Service. Control of both sorts was entrusted to the Treasury during the last century as part of the reforms that created a unified Civil Service recruited through open competition, and until 1919 these powers (except for questions of superannuation) were exercised by divisions also concerned with supply. At present separate sides of the Treasury are concerned with Supply and Establishments questions, except for three 'mixed' divisions that handle both.

Establishments control over numbers and grades is vested in five divisions. These are the three 'mixed' divisions, Government and Allied Services, Law and Order, and Imperial and Foreign, and two others, Establishments Departmental and Defence Personnel. Until 1939 this form of control was what it had been in the late nineteenth century. Departments were required to justify in advance each single variation in their complements. Not one additional clerk or cleaner was to be engaged by a department without Their Lordships' authority. Such detailed control could not be maintained in the face of the rapid and enormous expansion of departments during war-time. The Treasury accordingly delegated them a substantial degree of authority to vary complements without prior approval. But the post-war situation also, in view of the continuing great size and complexity of the Civil Service, made it impossible to reimpose the old restraints. Today, therefore, departments enjoy wide delegated powers to vary complements, subject to ceilings set by the Treasury. Each department is obliged to have in force a system for controlling its staff numbers. To supervise these systems and assist Establishments divisions in their annual comprehensive review of departmental complements, Staff Inspectors have been appointed with power to visit departments and make test checks of particular blocks of complements and staffs. The substance of the change remains: Treasury control has been relaxed and greater responsibility put on departments.

While the Treasury has relaxed in detail its control over complements and gradings, control over the second main branch of Establishments work, conditions of pay and service, remains absolute and comprehensive and, it may reasonably be argued, must so remain if a unified Civil Service is to be maintained. The responsibility of the divisions charged with these duties—Establishments General, Professional, Superannuation, and Manning—is to see that no changes are made in the code of pay or other conditions of service in any part of the Civil Service except on the initiative or with the concurrence of the Treasury.

To these two broad categories of Establishments business should be added a third, Organization and Methods. Repeated recommendations, going back as far as the MacDonnell Commission of 1912–14, led to the creation about 1920 of a small section to deal with such business and, particularly since the Second World War, to a very considerable expansion of those parts of the Establishments side concerned with administrative management, there now being an official with the rank of Under Secretary in charge of this work. Unlike the other Establishments divisions, O & M has no power of control over departments. Its decisions are advisory only, binding neither departments, nor for that matter other Establishments divisions whose control over complements and grading remains final.

II

THE CO-ORDINATION OF
FINANCIAL POLICY

TREASURY control in its classic form is exercised by the Supply divisions. Its purpose is co-ordination. This does not mean that Supply co-ordinates government policy as a whole and with regard to every aspect. Apart from the Cabinet, no unit of British government can claim so large a duty. Certainly no single body of officials could claim it—unless, perhaps, we take seriously the usage of those civil servants who lump together the Treasury, the Lord President's Office, and the Cabinet Office under the irreverent title of 'The Great George Street Front'. Upon the Supply divisions, however, rests the sufficiently comprehensive task of co-ordinating government policy so far as that policy has a financial aspect.

This means more than merely to prevent overlapping and inconsistency. It means so to control prospective expenditure as to achieve a balance in the programmes financed by that expenditure; or, in the words of R. G. Hawtrey, 'to secure a uniform standard in the measurement of the financial sacrifice involved in the activities

13

of all departments'.[1] The standard of balance is not one that can be more than approached in actual administration. Strictly, it would be satisfied only when expenditures were so distributed that the last pound spent on each programme produced the same amount of public good. In practice, it means that expenditure should not be extravagant in one sphere and parsimonious in another. Before it can be applied in making decisions it must also be informed by more concrete notions of policy, a set of priorities in terms of which services can be judged more or less necessary and expenditures extravagant or parsimonious—in short, some idea of public good. In British government the duty of fixing these priorities is vested in the Cabinet. Not the least service of a staff agency like the Treasury is that it brings together and presents for ministerial decision the questions that will elicit the statement of such a set of priorities. Supply thus has a role in the making as well as the execution of financial policy.

A government's financial policy has other aspects than that of balance among programmes of expenditure. The utilities and disutilities of expenditure and taxation must be weighed against one another. So also must the values of different kinds of taxation and borrowing. And in Britain today the general economic policy of the Government must also be considered when financial policy is

[1] R. G. Hawtrey, *The Exchequer and the Control of Expenditure* (London, 1921), pp. 28–29.

14

determined. With these aspects of financial policy other parts of the Treasury—in particular Home Finance, Overseas Finance, and Economic Affairs—are primarily concerned. But Supply officials are also aware of them and their hand in dealing with departmental expenditure is strengthened by the fact that they know and serve financial policy as a whole.

Where does economy stand among the purposes of Treasury control? If we mean by economy the policies which flowed from the high priority which Gladstonian finance assigned to leaving money 'to fructify in the pocket of the taxpayer'[1] then obviously this purpose has dwindled, although modern Chancellors, reasoning from quite different economic premises, may also demand a severe criticism of expenditure. In a larger sense, however, economy is inseparable from financial co-ordination. To prevent extravagance in one sphere in order to have more funds available for pressing needs elsewhere follows from the attempt to balance expenditure. So understood, and quite apart from what policy may directly imply, economy, now as in the past, remains a principal purpose of Treasury control and is enforced— if that is not too strong a word for describing how the Treasury deals with departments—along with the priorities of government policy.

[1] Bridges, *Treasury Control*, p. 7.

The requirement of prior approval

If these are the purposes of the control exercised by Supply, what is the scope of its powers and how does it go about exercising them? Its control does not consist solely of the review of the annual estimates. Still less does it imply anything resembling a comptroller's function. It is primarily a matter of what in Treasury usage is called 'week-to-week' or 'day-to-day' control. Briefly, it is a power obliging departments to obtain Treasury approval of any variation in departmental activity that has a financial aspect. That approval may be expressed in a specific sanction of a particular service or activity. It may also take the form of a general delegation, as when, for instance, the Treasury delegates to departments concerned with defence expenditure the authority to incur expenditure for new works, without seeking specific Treasury sanction, so long as the cost of any single project is not more than a specified amount. However approval may be expressed, it remains that no activity involving expenditure in the near or in the distant future can be undertaken by a department unless that activity has Treasury approval, and normally before the planning of any new activity has progressed very far Supply will have been consulted and its view obtained.

This power of day-to-day control has no specific statutory basis. Like much else in the ancient frame of British government, it is founded not on formal law, but on tradition and long acceptance. Nor is the statute book of much help in defining the scope of Treasury control. One indication can be found in the Exchequer and Audit Departments Act of 1866, a product of the great period of Gladstonian financial reform. This Act, as amended, states that whenever the Comptroller and Auditor General 'shall be required by the Treasury to ascertain whether any expenditure included in an appropriation account is supported by the authority of the Treasury, the Comptroller and Auditor General shall examine such expenditure with that object' and provides that if the Treasury does not see fit to sanction such 'unauthorized expenditure' as may be found, the expenditure 'shall be regarded as being not properly chargeable to a parliamentary grant'.[1] The Act does not create Treasury control, but assumes that it exists as a plenary power to control *all* expenditure. The Treasury has not, however, chosen to exercise this power to the full. Dating from 1868, the principal minute defining the scope of the power which the Treasury will exercise states that 'My Lords' consider that prior Treasury approval 'should be required for any increase of establishment, of salary, or of cost of a service, or for any additional works or new

---

[1] Sect. 1 (3), c. 52, 11 and 12 Geo. 5, *The Statutes, Third Revised Edition*, vol. xvi, 1918–21, London, 1950. The original language of the Act of 1866, which is not materially different, can be found in Sect. 27, chap. xxxiv, pp. 424 ff., *The Statutes of the United Kingdom of Great Britain and Ireland*, by George Kettilby Rickards, vol. xxvii, London, 1866.

services which have not been specially provided for in the grants of Parliament'.[1] Quite inconsistent with this definition is a later authoritative description in a Treasury minute of 1914 stating 'the general practice of the Treasury' as being 'to require Treasury sanction for all expenditure' except for 'particular categories of expenditure of a special character'.[2] The fact of the matter, well understood in the Treasury and in departments, is that, while the Supply divisions will centre their attention largely on proposed new services, recurrent services and expenditures drop out of their control only as the Treasury permits them to.

Even when we turn to those proposals requiring prior approval, Treasury practice can hardly be reduced to rule. Precisely what types of proposal do or do not require prior approval? The criteria have never been codified. Later minutes and letters have done much to define the terms of the minute of 1868 and the extent to which departments may incur expenditure without prior approval. The substance of the principal instructions can be found in the *Epitome* of the reports of the Public Accounts Committee which is compiled at infrequent intervals. Here can be found, for instance, illustrations of what the Treasury understands by that difficult term 'a new service'. Here also are examples of letters from

[1] *Epitome of the Reports from the Committees of Public Accounts 1857–1937* (Parliamentary Papers, 1937–8, vol. xxii), pp. 20–21.
[2] *Epitome* (Treasury Minute 8 December 1914, par. 7), p. 565.

the Treasury to departments delegating to them authority to incur expenditure on additional works under certain circumstances and within a certain monetary limit and evidence for the rule that a lump-sum estimate does not relieve a department from obtaining approval for the specific 'services' on which the funds covered by the estimate will be spent. Here in the detail of particular decisions of particular cases precision and substance are given to the general doctrine of prior Treasury approval.

To the *Epitome* Treasury officials, when dealing with questions raised before the Public Accounts Committee, may refer for authoritative guidance. Otherwise, however, it is not much used and generally in day-to-day administration there is relatively little reliance on any formal instructions or written source as governing the relations of departments and Supply divisions. A departmental finance officer, for example, may refer to the phrases of the minute of 1868 and may be guided by a 'rude letter' written to him or a predecessor in the name of Their Lordships on some occasion when the department had offended. But he acknowledges the authority of such explicit propositions as part of a context which contains many unwritten and even unspoken elements. The operative principles are more like standards of professional conduct than formal rules of law.

It all sounds very British: the avoidance of definite rules, the reliance on tradition and 'common sense'. But does this not leave the whole matter much too vague for successful administration? One test is the opinion of those who are subject to the Treasury's power, the departmental officials. And they, if they do have complaints against the Treasury, do not make unpredictability or the vagueness of its requirements one of them. The fact is that to attempt to codify such a subtle complex of administrative practice as Treasury control would very probably gravely distort it. Precisely for reasons of smooth and predictable administration, it is better to rely—in the manner of the common law—upon tradition and common understanding than upon codification.

Criticism of new legislation and policy

The requirement of prior approval is the principal foundation of the Treasury's power to co-ordinate financial policy. Given Cabinet policy, the Treasury's position in bringing balance into government programmes through its criticism of departmental expenditure is unassailable—assuming, of course, that Treasury officials understand that policy as do ministers and that ministers cannot be prevailed upon to reverse themselves. But Cabinet policy, of course, is not always 'given'. It is continually being formed, modified, extended, even when its main lines are held constant over a period. In this there is a potential threat to Treasury control. Suppose, for instance, that a minister sets his heart strongly on some scheme which he has good reason to suspect the Treasury would reject as being out of line with government policy. He therefore takes his proposal straight to the Cabinet where he may win its acceptance, perhaps without thorough examination of its relation to existing policy. If so, the Treasury will have been by-passed and will be obliged to approve any new services involved by the scheme. In the actual world of administration the Treasury's power to require prior approval would be gravely impaired if it did not also firmly possess the further right to criticize proposals of new policy before they reach the Cabinet level.

The Chancellor's constitutional responsibility for finance should in itself suffice to ensure that the Treasury has this opportunity. He should be able, that is, to delay a decision by the Cabinet until his officials have prepared a brief. From the nature of day-to-day Treasury control, it also follows that ordinarily a proposal involving finance will have been discussed between the Treasury and the department at a very early stage. Reinforcing these means of protection are the rules of Cabinet procedure providing that normally no proposal shall be placed upon the Cabinet agenda until an appropriate memorandum has previously been circulated among Cabinet members and that, where questions of finance are involved, no proposal shall be circulated until the sanction of the Chancellor of the Exchequer has been obtained to its circulation.[1] The purpose of the

---

[1] Sir W. Ivor Jennings, *Cabinet Government*, 2nd edn. (Cambridge, 1951), pp. 139 and 228–9.

latter rule is not to give the Chancellor a veto over what measures may be brought before the Cabinet or Cabinet Committee—given the nature of the Cabinet, he could not maintain the power even if he were formally given it. The purpose is rather to ensure that there has been proper examination by officials of the departments concerned before the questions are put to ministers for decision, and one effect is to ensure that Supply has the opportunity to point out the financial consequences, as well as possible conflicts with other existing policies or activities. Here Supply acts as a staff agency advising the executive in the formation of policy. But this function is inseparable from its role as co-ordinator. Supply's control over new services and additional expenditure could not in practice be maintained effectively without this further power.

Supported by these sanctions—the requirement of prior approval and the opportunity to criticize proposed new legislation and policy—the business of control goes on continuously throughout the year. The general form of the procedure followed may be briefly sketched. Suppose, for instance, that a department seeks approval for some scheme—the repair or construction of a bridge; the drainage of certain agricultural land in the Highlands; a subsidy for experimental types of civilian aircraft or to an hotel owner with plans for attracting dollar tourists; the bulk purchase of the West African cocoa crop; a plan to provide soldiers on leave with cheap motoring. A request for approval may be initiated in a personal letter from the Accountant General or from the departmental administrative officer concerned to the head of the appropriate Supply division, from whom, when a decision has been reached, a letter of approval constitutes evidence of Treasury sanction. Before the initiating letter is dispatched, however, there will probably have been much consultation, and throughout—such is the actual procedure in most matters of daily concern—the discussions will have been conducted and the decision made by one of the Principals in the division. In the great mass of cases approval is given without difficulty. Sometimes, however, there is a negative reply from the Treasury and occasionally a 'row', when the question will be referred on up the lines of hierarchy in the Treasury and the department, the ultimate arbiter being, of course, the Cabinet.

Consultation between the Treasury and a department may mean as little as a telephone conversation between two officials. It may mean a meeting, or several meetings, of a number of officials from departments and the Treasury, who, if the question is one continuing in importance for some time, may be constituted as an *ad hoc* committee. It may mean—particularly if the question relates to new legislation or policy—discussion by one of the standing interdepartmental committees of officials established to deal with certain large aspects of public policy and on which the Treasury will almost

WORKING MEN'S
COLLEGE
LIBRARY

always have a regular representative. The result may be agreement with or without modification of the proposal —and, as we shall see, there are within the British system strong pressures toward agreement at the official level. In the event of disagreement the Treasury will have had the chance to examine the matter from its own and departmental aspects and will provide the Chancellor or other Treasury minister with a brief to be used when the question comes before ministers. The system ensures that when ministers make policy decisions the staff work needed to prepare for them will have been done.

Through such decisions made at the ministerial level by the Cabinet or Cabinet committees, officials are continuously kept informed of Government policy. There are other means by which officials keep in touch with policy—for example, the Chancellor's Budget Speech, the *Economic Survey*, White Papers such as those on the Defence Programme, and, in general, ministerial statements of policy in Parliament. If, however, one asks officials how they know what Government policy is, the main stress of the replies will be on the decisions made or confirmed as 'papers pass up and down' the Treasury hierarchy.

Priorities in defence and civil expenditure

In exercising the day-to-day control which follows from the requirement of prior approval, Treasury officials shape departmental initiative to accord with Government policy. In this process, however, policy is not only applied. By proposing new expenditure, as by proposing new legislation, departments may raise questions which may lead to the making of new policy. Government policy matures throughout the year, rather than being unchangeably fixed for a given period at a particular time. There are, however, occasions when a general review of policy is undertaken and decisions are made laying down the main lines of action for some time to come. Of these the framing of the Budget is undoubtedly the most important. Since it is the culmination of a series of decisions on economic, as well as financial policy, it can best be examined after we have considered the co-ordination of economic policy. One stage in this series, however, is the decision on the general pattern of expenditure for the coming year, and in the making of this decision Supply plays an important part and exercises a further form of control. It does this principally through its annual review of the estimates of departmental expenditure which are submitted to the Treasury before going to Parliament. Closely related to this review is a preceding decision which greatly affects the general pattern of expenditure and which has a certain parallel in the annual 'preview' of expenditure in American budgeting.

In American government there is nothing really comparable to the most important form of Treasury control, the requirement of prior approval. Treasury criticism of proposals of new legislation bears some likeness to the work of legislative reference performed by the Bureau of the Budget, while in the United States, as in Britain, the review of the estimates, although quite differently conducted, is a means of co-ordinating policy as well as enforcing economy. Also, in the United States, before calling for departmental estimates, the Bureau of the Budget makes a 'preview' of expenditure and revenue which leads to the setting of tentative ceilings on certain types of expenditure by Presidential authority. Rather similarly in Britain, the Chancellor, with the aid of the Treasury and in consultation with the ministers concerned, determines, in advance of the annual review of the estimates, the relative orders of magnitude which he proposes for different sections of government expenditure. As in the United States, the largest section is defence expenditure, which because of its importance in recent years and because its control differs in some ways from that of civil expenditure, deserves special attention.

The departments concerned are the three service ministries, the Ministry of Defence, and the Ministry of Supply, a substantial part of whose expenditure is reckoned as defence expenditure. Over much of the expenditure of these departments the Defence Matériel Division of the Treasury exercises the usual form of day-to-day control. Throughout the year many proposals involving new works, or new services of production or of research and development, are submitted to it for prior approval and the usual give and take occurs between Supply and departmental officials. A great deal of new defence expenditure may be included in the estimates, however, which has not been so criticized and controlled. This figure will depend upon the total provision for defence agreed on by the Chancellor and the Minister of Defence and the Service Ministers. Upon the Minister of Defence falls the burden of allocating this provision among the Services, although, of course, the implications of that allocation are bound themselves to enter into consideration when the total figure for defence is being discussed.

It results from this procedure that the Services and the Ministry of Supply will put together for presentation to Parliament estimates which will include projects which have not yet been fully worked out or submitted to Treasury criticism. That criticism will, however, take place, for even after the estimates have gone to Parliament the defence departments will, as their plans for these projects develop, submit them to the Treasury, whose aim, however, will be not so much to reduce total expenditure as to get the best value for a sum already agreed upon.

How effectively can Supply officials criticize defence expenditure? Many proposals, of course, can be examined in the light of the practice and experience of other departments. Proposals of new works, for instance, may involve the construction of buildings not greatly different in character and use from some commonly put up by civil departments or by local authorities. Where works or services serve special defence purposes—for instance, the development or production of new weapons—criticism is more difficult. But even when Supply officials do not have the technical knowledge needed to judge the details of a proposal, they can perform a useful service by 'asking questions', requiring defence officials to explain, for instance, why they propose so large an expenditure on one scheme rather than another, which on the face of it may seem equally important.

Still, as the form of the procedure indicates, the criticism of defence expenditure is more difficult than that of civil expenditure, and many decisions, which in the latter sphere would emerge from the business of day-to-day control, in the former follow from the comprehensive decision on the total provision for defence. Such a decision must be ministerial, flowing in the main from the Government's estimate of the strategic situation and the danger of war. In the discussions from which these decisions emerge the Chancellor will, of course, take his part, being concerned especially with the economic implications of a given level of defence expenditure, i.e. its bearing on inflation, the balance of payments, particular sections of the export industries, and so on. But there is nothing to prevent him from plunging into discussion of the largest strategic questions and, if recent Chancellors have behaved as did their predecessors, they have not been reticent in urging their views on these matters as well as on finance and economics.

The procedure of an annual preview adopted in respect of defence expenditure applies also, though in more general terms, to civil expenditure. Here, too, the Chancellor's daily contacts with his colleagues will have provided him with a view of the financial provisions which they are likely to need in the following year, and he will be able to indicate, at a relatively early stage in the annual formulation of financial policy, how far he considers such expenditure to be feasible, having regard to the condition of the economy and the importance of balance among various categories of expenditure. He must attempt, for example, to weigh the claims of the National Health Service against the needs of agriculture, to measure the demands of education against the appeal for better roads and a more expansive policy for civil aviation. He must endeavour to help both his colleagues and his own officials by suggesting an equitable balance between these conflicting interests and the proportions in which, in his view, they would most fairly share among themselves the limited sum of expenditure which can be tolerated.

The need as well as the difficulty of maintaining such a general control over expenditure was sharply illustrated during the early days of the Health Service when actual expenditure continued to soar well beyond original and revised expectations. As a result, in March 1950, Sir

Stafford Cripps, although in the midst of his 'austerity drive', and although he had previously given the House what looked very much like an assurance that there would be no more such supplementary estimates, was obliged to ask for a further £98 million for the Health Service in the current financial year.[1]

While it is the responsibility of the Chancellor to indicate such priorities in civil expenditure, by the nature of Cabinet government his decision cannot be final and beyond all appeal. If the other minister or ministers concerned disagree, it is always open to them to appeal the question to the Cabinet where a trial of strength with the Chancellor will take place, its outcome being determined by personal and political factors as well as the institutional authority of the various combatants. With regard to defence expenditure, such disagreements and consequent struggles within the Cabinet occurred before both world wars.[2] In recent years, however, decisions seem to have been more easily arrived at, opinion with regard to defence policy among officials as well as ministers having moved very much in unison.

The principal exception, of course, would be the conflict which led to the resignation of Mr. Bevan in 1951.

[1] 472 H.C. Deb. 916 ff. (14 March 1950). In his Budget Speech of the previous year, Cripps gave this assurance: 'I have emphasized that only in special cases, such as, for example, major changes of policy, can any supplementary estimates in future be permitted.' 463 H.C. Deb. 2084 (6 April 1949).

[2] W. S. Churchill, *The World Crisis* (London, 1923), vol. i, pp. 172–8; *The Gathering Storm* (Boston, 1948), p. 126.

It seems that the main issue between him and Mr. Gaitskell, then Chancellor of the Exchequer, was the provision to be made for the Health Service. 'The Chancellor of the Exchequer', said Mr. Bevan when explaining his resignation to the House, 'is putting a financial ceiling on the Health Service.'[1] At issue also, however, was the increase in defence expenditure which Mr. Gaitskell, taking a position not always familiar to Chancellors of the Exchequer, advocated against his Cabinet colleague. Failing to carry the Cabinet on these questions, Mr. Bevan chose to resign rather than to accept the collective decision.

May we regard this business of fixing priorities for certain broad types of expenditure as a form of Treasury control? It involves decisions by ministers, perhaps even by the Cabinet. But so may the issues raised by the business of day-to-day control. The interesting question is how far the Treasury—ministers as well as officials—can be guided by the notion of balance in making or recommending decisions. Is it possible to weigh rationally the claims of such expenditure against other competing claims? The difficulties are obvious. Is not the value of national defence infinite? How can any other service, private or public, compare with the need for survival? And almost as inestimable is the value of the health programme: does it not save lives?

These questions raise nice problems in the logic of

[1] 487 H.C. Deb. 41 (23 April 1951).

31

choice. But whether or not there is, strictly speaking, a rational way of making such decisions, the Treasury does try to achieve a balance with regard to these sorts of expenditure as well as others. After the outbreak of the Korean War, for instance, it was generally agreed among officials and ministers that the danger of world war within a year or two was greatly heightened. The defence programme therefore was reassessed and economic planners were asked to estimate in the light of its impact on the balance of payments and certain other assumptions, such as the expected level of American aid, what was the maximum defence expenditure that the economy could bear. From these calculations issued the increases in the defence proposals leading to the three-year programme announced in January of the following year.[1] Without pressing the point too far, one can say that the general pattern of expenditure resulting from this readjustment of priorities did, in a real sense, reflect an effort to weigh the value of defence against other national needs.

Annual review of estimates

Within the general framework of this assessment of priorities as between the main classes of expenditure, the more detailed pattern of expenditure, new and old, is determined mainly by means of the annual review of the

[1] 483 H.C. Deb. 581 ff. (29 January 1951). See also the White Paper on defence, Cmd. 8146, and the debate on it, 14–15 February 1951. 484 H.C. Deb. 410 ff.

estimates. This is 'the time'—in the words of a Chancellor—'when the expenditure of the Departments and the numbers of their staffs are examined as a whole'.[1] In recent years the Treasury has also received from departments, twice a year, estimates of their probable expenditure for two years ahead. These help prevent expenditure from getting out of hand, and when interpreted in the light of economic forecasts may lead to a change in policy. The receipt of one of these sets of long-range estimates coincides with the annual review of the estimates, enlarging the perspective from which they may be criticized.

The procedure followed in reviewing the estimates can be briefly sketched. Early in October the Treasury sends out a circular to the civil departments asking them to send in their estimates for the following year by the beginning of December. Received in the Treasury by an official known as the Estimate Clerk, these estimates are forwarded by him to the appropriate divisions, subheads for Establishments or Supply divisions being considered respectively by Establishments or Supply divisions, except, of course, in the case of those going to the mixed divisions. Review is conducted, not as in the United States at hearings before which departments appear, but within the divisions, which consult with departments as they find it necessary. After review the divisions return the estimates to the Estimate Clerk, recommending

---

[1] 493 H.C. Deb. 202 (7 November 1951).

approval either at the stated figure or with modifications. Thence they are submitted to Treasury ministers, and in February and March they are published and presented to the House of Commons by the Financial Secretary. While this is the procedure followed for the civil estimates, those for the fighting services must also be approved by the Treasury. These, however, are considered in terms of rather broader categories of expenditure and, reflecting this fact, their presentation to the House is made by the departmental ministers concerned.

The whole business of compiling and reviewing the estimates is done far more quickly than in the United States. There the call for departmental estimates goes out in June, twelve months before the beginning of the financial year with which they are concerned. In September they are received by the Budget Bureau where they are reviewed and from which they are sent to Congress four months later. In Britain estimates are formally asked for about six months before the start of the financial year, departments taking some two months to get them to the Treasury which devotes about the same length of time to their review. Not only is the business got through quickly, it is also done with a relatively small staff. The Trade and Industry Division, for instance, handles all supply questions, including review of the estimates, of three of the larger and more important departments—the Board of Trade, the Ministry of Fuel and Power, and the Ministry of Transport and Civil Aviation—as well as the civil side of the Ministry of Supply. It has, however, a complement of only five—one Assistant Secretary, two Principals, one Temporary Administrative Assistant, one Executive Officer—and a clerical section of two or three. The working force of the Supply divisions, including mixed divisions, numbers around fifty, exclusive of clerical staff. Before the reorganization of 1951—we may note for the sake of a rough comparison—the Estimates division of the Budget Bureau had a staff of some 150, excluding secretaries and secretarial help.

Financial powers of the executive

The estimates are primarily a means of providing Parliament with an opportunity for the control of government expenditure. The freedom of action which they leave to the executive, however, is very great—much greater than that enjoyed by the American executive. Against the misuse of these wide powers, Treasury control is a major safeguard, providing a complement or balance on the administrative plane to the powerful position of the executive under Cabinet government. Three questions will help bring out this function of Treasury control: What is the bearing of prior approval upon the estimates? How strictly do the estimates bind the executive? Under what parliamentary limitations may the executive incur liabilities committing it to future expenditure?

The answer to the first question will again emphasize

the large powers of the Treasury over all departmental activities so far as they involve expenditure in the present or the future. In part these powers may be expressed through Treasury control of the estimates. That a proposal has been sanctioned by the Treasury in the course of its day-to-day control does not entail automatic approval at the time of the annual review of the estimates. Then, regardless of the previous action, provision for the service may be reduced or excluded from the estimates, such a power being, of course, indispensable if the pattern of expenditure as a whole is to be effectively reviewed. But, while prior approval does not entail approval of an estimate, neither does approval of an estimate dispense with the requirement of prior approval, which remains the most important single form of Treasury control. By Treasury instruction, supported by the Act of 1866, that sanction must be given separately and no new service may be included in the estimates submitted by a department to Supply unless prior approval has been granted, or in case of urgency, unless concurrently Treasury authority is applied for.

Ordinarily, then, before a department includes a new service or other matter needing approval in its estimates, it will have submitted the proposal to the Treasury, consultations will have been held, and sanction will have been given. When it comes to the review of the estimates, therefore, Supply is not likely to be confronted with proposals which it has not already considered. Rather similarly in the United States there is a good deal of informal consultation before the various divisions of the Bureau of the Budget hold their annual hearings in review of estimates. Like the process of granting prior approval, these consultations facilitate the business of review. There, however, the similarity ends. Informal as the consultations which lead to the granting of prior approval may be in Britain, it is of the essence that they should culminate in a formal sanction, a letter stating that approval has been given, which the Comptroller and Auditor General under the terms of the Act of 1866 will require the department to possess.

In exercising its power to require prior approval the Treasury will demand far more detailed information about proposed expenditure than is given in the estimates. What is more important, this control also extends into the future. While the estimates cover only expenditure which will be incurred during the coming financial year, prior approval must be obtained for proposals although they involve expenditure only in later years. Before it incurs liabilities, as well as before it incurs expenditure, a department must obtain Treasury sanction. This power, going well beyond that expressed in the review of the estimates, is indispensable to the orderly exercise of the executive's wide powers in the sphere of expenditure.

How far are these powers of the executive limited by the estimates? How strictly do the estimates bind the

WORKING MEN'S
COLLEGE
LIBRARY

Government and the Treasury once they have been sanctioned by Supply and voted by Parliament? If we ask these questions of American government, we raise an ancient and stubborn problem of the Federal budgeting process. This is the problem of the specific appropriation, stating in detail the objects for which money may be spent, or what comes to the same thing, the presentation to appropriations sub-committees of detailed estimates informally but effectively committing the agency to a specific programme of expenditure of lump-sum appropriations. The criticism of these practices is familiar. They greatly add to the work of compiling departmental and the Executive budgets, drawing out the length of the budgeting process. They may oblige agencies to estimate expenditure in a detail which the inevitable contingencies of the future make unrealistic and in budget execution often gravely restrict the freedom of decision needed by both the President and agencies if financial policy is to be efficient and economical.[1] Does a similar problem arise in Britain?

Certainly the estimates as submitted to Parliament go into considerable detail.[2] Those for the fighting services

[1] See Arthur Smithies, *The Budgetary Process in the United States* (New York, 1955), ch. iii; and Arthur W. Macmahon, 'Congressional Oversight of Administration: The Power of the Purse', *Pol. Sci. Quarterly*, June and September 1943.

[2] Each estimate is divided into three parts: Part I, which alone is reproduced in the Appropriation Act, provides the statutory description of the purpose for which the supply requested in the estimates is ultimately granted. Part II shows the subheads under which the

consist of some 34 Votes—about the same in number as the appropriations of the U.S. Defense Department—those for the civil services of 150 or so Votes, in each set the Votes being further subdivided into subheads and items, the latter sometimes including two degrees of detail. The subheads setting out salaries for personal services are as minutely specific as the comparable headings in American Budgets before 1950,[1] while 'Works in Progress' are described down to the name and location and cost of each project—a temporary garage and workshop at a post office in Hull, the adaptation of a building to provide office accommodation in Hereford.

What other information does Parliament receive concerning the expenditure proposed in the estimates? While it does not receive 'justifications' explaining the estimates in detail as do American appropriations committees, certain explanatory documents are submitted. There is a memorandum on the civil estimates, running to perhaps a hundred pages—not, however, a very informative document—and separate and rather more detailed memoranda from each of the fighting service departments. A financial statement consisting of tables relating to revenue, expenditure, the national debt, &c., is submitted when the Chancellor makes his Budget

Treasury, acting under Section 23 of the Exchequer and Audit Departments Act, 1866, requires departments to account for expenditure. Part III gives further details for the information of Parliament.

[1] See Smithies, *The Budgetary Process*, pp. 83 ff.

Speech in which he expounds his general financial policy at the start of a debate of several days' length. During the debates on the estimates, the more particular policies of departments provide the subjects, but not all departments and only a fraction of all programmes are considered. Certain estimates are examined intensively by the Select Committee on Estimates; it is concerned not with policy, however, but with economy and administrative management, and its reports are made too late in the session to influence the estimates of the current year. In general, while Parliament is well informed about policy, it lacks the full and detailed information relating to proposed expenditure which is normally made available to American appropriations committees. British parliamentary procedure does not provide for the kind of thorough examination of both policy and management that may be made at hearings before these committees. Lacking also is the opportunity, which these hearings present, for legislators to induce officials informally to commit their agencies to specific items and patterns of expenditures.

This does not mean, however, that the British executive is free to spend funds as it likes, subject only to the limitations imposed by the Acts appropriating them. In Britain, as in the United States, Appropriation Acts omit much of the detail included in the statements of estimates submitted to the legislature. The annual Appropriation Act enumerates only the Votes and the Classes in which, in the case of the civil estimates, the Votes are grouped. Legally, therefore, the executive is not bound by the sub-heads and items of the original estimates, although since the general 'ambit' of each Vote is delimited in the Act, expenditure cannot be shifted from one Vote to another.

This legal freedom, however, is limited by important safeguards. The first is that departments may deviate from the subheads of an estimate in order to use savings on one subhead to cover excesses on another only with express Treasury sanction. Along with its power to require prior approval, to review the annual estimates, and to examine financial proposals before they go to ministers, this power to authorize transfers of expenditure between subheads constitutes an important form of Treasury control. Like the power to require prior approval it rests upon tradition rather than statute. It is also limited by tradition—by an informal commitment of the Treasury to the Parliament that it will be used to authorize transfers only in certain cases. Regarding these limits the Treasury deprecates any attempt to lay down 'too precise a definition in general terms'.[1] It has, how-

[1] *Epitome*, p. 622, Treasury Minute 24 November 1921 on 3rd Report, PAC, 1921. To the Public Accounts Committee, which had been critical of certain instances in which the Treasury had exercised the power to authorize virement, the Treasury replied, '. . . while the Estimates in most cases contain, for the information of Parliament, a subdivision of these totals into various subheads, these subheads are not as such voted by Parliament. Within the total of a Vote—which cannot be exceeded without Parliamentary authority—and provided that no expenditure is incurred which does not fall within

ever, told departments that 'savings on subheads which are largely unrelated to the general run of the Vote will not be regarded as available to meet excesses elsewhere on the Vote'.[1] In any given case the Treasury decides whether the proposed new expenditure is of such importance or so great a departure from the original items in the estimate as to require to be brought specially before Parliament.

In the case of the fighting services, where accurate estimation is particularly hard and the need for flexibility great, a special degree of freedom is allowed. While the departments concerned, and the Treasury as well, are bound by the terms of the Votes included in the civil estimates, a service department may go beyond the terms of its Votes, transferring surpluses from one to another. It can, however, do this only with Treasury approval and since such a transfer would otherwise contravene the terms of the Appropriation Act, that Act annually grants this power to the Treasury, requiring that such transfers be reported to Parliament and receive subsequent parliamentary sanction, regularly given in a later Appropriation Act.

This power of authorizing transfers between subheads

the ambit of the wording of the Appropriation Act passed by Parliament, *discretion has always and, in their Lordships' opinion, must always be given to the Executive if the business of Government is to be carried on.* The exercise of that discretion is vested in the Treasury, not in the actual spending Department' (p. 621). [My italics.]   [1] 4th Report, PAC, 1950–1, p. 6.

or Service Votes—the power of 'virement'—the Treasury retains as an element of its control. To the departments on their own authority are left transfers from one item to another. Considering the breadth of some of the sub-heads, this may seem a considerable power. But where a subhead contains a large sum it is usually all allocated to one specific type of payment. And where a subhead contains a multiplicity of items, either the total sum is small, or the items themselves are statutory payments not easily variable by the department, or they reflect types of expenditure which are understood to be subject to the requirement of prior Treasury approval even though the scales of payment themselves are not actually controlled by the Treasury. Nor does this system of trans-fers relieve departments of the need to take pains to be as accurate as possible in programming expenditure. The appropriation accounts, in which departments account for expenditure under subheads as well as Votes, will reveal over- or under-estimation, which may subject responsible officials to criticism by the Treasury and the Public Accounts Committee.

Like the American executive, the British executive is informally restricted within limits far narrower than the terms of the Appropriation Acts. These limits, however, are not set, as is very often the case in the United States, by commitments to specific expenditures arising from particular understandings with individual legislators and legislative committees (see Smithies, op. cit., p. 138).

While not precise, the limits on the British executive are set by an accepted general rule and within them the executive enjoys the wide area of manœuvre given it by the recognized power of virement. As a result the British executive, in comparison with the American, has greater freedom of action, which it may use to make economies and correct normal discrepancies in the estimation of expenditure. At the same time, Parliament retains control over policy, as it is reflected in the estimates, to which purposes alone government expenditure is restricted. These arrangements, it is true, also mean that Parliament does not exercise control over the details of expenditure as the American Congress often does. But that power would hardly be compatible with Cabinet government.

As a rule the British executive may incur expenditure only for the purposes covered by estimates voted by Parliament. It is, however, worth noting an exception which makes it possible for a department to incur, for a limited period, expenditure not so covered. Suppose that ministers have decided to inaugurate a new service or find themselves confronted by a substantial underestimate of the cost of an existing service. Funds to cover such contingencies must be obtained from Parliament by means of a supplementary estimate. The disadvantages of delay or disruption of the service, however, are avoided by the fact that although the estimate has not yet been voted by Parliament, the Treasury may sanction the expenditure involved. It will not do this unless a supplementary is submitted in the same financial year as the expenditure is incurred. Since, however, the last supplementaries are normally submitted only a little more than a month before the close of the financial year, this requirement is not a serious inconvenience.

Power of the executive to incur liabilities

In its freedom to incur liabilities the British executive also enjoys what must seem from the American point of view an even more remarkable power. The point can be brought out if we examine a peculiarity about the estimates presented to, and the appropriations voted by, the British Parliament. It is that they show only the sums which are expected actually to come in course of payment during the year to which they relate. They include cash required to meet liabilities outstanding at the end of the previous year and cash required to meet new liabilities incurred and coming into payment in the current year. They do not, however, provide for liabilities which may be incurred in the current year, but which do not come into payment until a later year. In short, appropriations in Britain do not present that familiar feature of recent American budgets: a discrepancy, sometimes huge, between the sum that will actually be spent in the financial year and the sum appropriated, which will be spent over a period of years. The reason for the American practice is obvious: many programmes, especially defence programmes, can be carried out only over a period of years; hence, if departments are to make the necessary commitments they must be assured of the requisite appropriations. But the British Government also undertakes activities of this kind; it also has a set of long-run defence programmes. How does it avoid the discrepancy?

The reason in a nutshell is that while in Britain the executive can, if circumstances are sufficiently compelling, incur liabilities not already covered by an appropriation, in the United States it cannot. Exceptions to the rule occur in the United States when Congress from time to time specifically provides in legislation that a department, for a limited period and within a fixed sum, may make contracts creating liabilities not covered by an appropriation. The general rule, however, is that if a department of the Federal Government is legally to incur liabilities, even though they do not come in payment during the current year, these liabilities must already be covered by an appropriation. Freed of this limitation, the British executive in launching a programme is obliged to ask Parliament only for such funds as appear to be needed for the fiscal year, the result being that appropriations and expenditure are not greatly discrepant.

Historically, of course, supply came to be granted for only a year at a time as a means of giving Parliament a tighter control over the Crown. The Crown, however, retained the power, which the American executive has never had, to incur liabilities not covered by an appropriation or contract authorization. Of course, in a political sense, the President may 'incur liabilities' or 'make commitments' without such authority. He might, for instance, commit the United States to providing economic or military aid to a foreign country, although Congress had not yet appropriated or authorized the necessary funds. But the American executive could not legally make contracts to procure the goods needed to fulfil such commitments, while in a similar situation the British executive could. Regularly, British officials, on behalf of the executive, make legally binding contracts which involve the future payment of sums which are not yet covered by estimates presented to, nor appropriations voted by, Parliament.[1]

Peculiar as it must seem in American eyes, this power,

[1] Such an agreement—e.g. a contract arranging for the rental over a period of years of a piece of land for some government installation —will provide for payments in future years, although no appropriation to cover these payments has yet been made. Furthermore, it will not include language which makes the payment of such sums conditional upon their being voted by Parliament. What if at a later date the Government decides to discontinue the activity from which the agreement sprang? In such an event the department will negotiate a compromise financial settlement and Parliament will be asked to provide the necessary funds.

Once the power of the British executive so to incur liabilities has been made clear, the safeguards need immediately to be pointed out. The principal one is, of course, that if the Government makes a commitment of importance it will inform Parliament of what it is doing at the earliest possible opportunity. Furthermore, actual we may also observe, is necessary if the British system of annual audits is to work effectively. That system has often been admired and it has been proposed that something similar be imported into American government. Such proposals necessarily include the requirement that appropriations be made only for the current year in order that the audit shall be timely. But inconvenient as that would be in 'normal' times, it would be virtually impossible when the Government is pushing ahead with great programmes of expenditure like those of recent defence budgets—unless Congress were ready to grant the executive a power to incur liabilities comparable with that enjoyed by the British executive. Conceivably this could be done by greatly extending the present limited practice of granting the executive the power to make contracts to be covered by later appropriations. Otherwise, American government cannot avail itself of the much-praised system of an annual audit. And only if these contract authorizations were in fairly general terms would the freedom of decision left the executive be comparable to that enjoyed by the British executive.

The wider power of the British as compared with the American executive in incurring liabilities consists not only in this freedom with regard to appropriations. The British executive also is less restricted by the need for

expenditure upon such commitments obviously depends upon Parliament's sanctioning in due course the charge on public funds.

statutory sanction. In the United States, because of the rules of the House of Representatives, Appropriation Bills are not normally proceeded with unless the expenditure which they are to cover has already been authorized by law,[1] and such authorizations, often in the form of permanent legislation, sometimes in the form of annual legislation, themselves commonly set limits on the amount that may be expended.

To what extent does the British executive need statutory sanction in order to incur liabilities? It is a recognized feature of British practice that any Bill introduced into Parliament, the carrying out of which will involve a charge on public funds, should be accompanied by a separate financial resolution, the purpose of which is to make clear to Parliament the financial implications of the measure. That resolution must be recommended by the Crown and voted by the House of Commons, sitting in Committee, before the statute itself can come into effect. Between it and the authorizations passed by the American Congress there is a certain similarity. It should be pointed out, however, that a financial resolution will not always set a specific limit to the charge which the Act imposes on public funds. In some cases, where a new service is established and is intended to be carried on by a department as part of its ordinary continuing business —for instance, the National Health Service—the determination of the amounts to be provided is left to be dealt

---

[1] Rule XXI, cl. 2, *Rules of the House of Representatives.*

WORKING MEN'S
COLLEGE
LIBRARY

with by the annual estimates procedure. In other cases, where, for any reason, it may be desirable to fix some limit to the amount of public money which may be spent before the policy must be resubmitted to Parliament in a new Bill—for instance, subsidies to the film industry— a specific total will be named in the financial resolution and in the Bill. In any case, of course, the passage of the resolution, like American authorizations, is quite distinct from the appropriation of funds to cover the expenditure on the service.

The interesting point, when one is making compari- sons with American practice, is that in some spheres the British executive can incur liabilities for activities which do not have the statutory sanction provided by the finan- cial resolution procedure. Ultimately, of course, the cash to cover annual expenditure on these activities will be provided by an Appropriation Act, and in this sense and in this form statutory sanction must at some point be received. Liabilities may be incurred, however, not only before the appropriation has been made but also in the absence of a statute embodying a financial resolution. Just what activities enjoy this privileged position is a question which has from time to time agitated the Comp- troller and Auditor General and the Public Accounts Committee. It is at any rate unquestioned that activities required for the defence of the realm—e.g. letting con- tracts for ships, aeroplanes, and other large munitions of war—are so privileged, and in this sphere both the law of the constitution and constitutional 'propriety' permit the executive to incur liabilities extending over a period of years, although the activities concerned do not have statutory sanction. It has also been argued that civil departments enjoy a less wide but similar privilege. And it has happened that civil departments have not only incurred liabilities for services lacking statutory authority but have even incurred liabilities involving expenditure exceeding the limits on expenditure set by statute. Underlying these powers and the problems they raise is the retention by the Crown of powers founded not on statute but on constitutional custom—in short, the remaining powers of the ancient prerogative.[1]

[1] For discussion of this whole question see *Epitome* (1857–1937), pp. 85, 264, 468, 724; PAC 1912, Evidence, Q. 3427–42; and especially PAC 2nd Report, 1932, par. 3, and Evidence, Q. 840–1, 853; also Erskine May, *Parliamentary Practice* (15th edn.), p. 726. In summary: (1) For defence purposes the executive may incur liabilities extending over a period of years, although these activities do not have statutory sanction. (2) It also seems agreed that civil as well as defence departments may in some cases incur liabilities for services without statutory sanction when these liabilities are incurred and fall due within a single financial year and which, therefore, will be covered by an appropriation voted during that year. (3) Civil departments have also incurred continuing liabilities for continuing services which do not have statutory sanction, but their action has been questioned by the Comptroller and Auditor General and criticized by the Public Accounts Committee. (4) The Treasury, while agreeing that normally statutory sanction should be sought for the continuing services of civil departments, has insisted that there are exceptions. Its position has been that from the point of view of law, (*a*) a service may be sufficiently authorized by the Appropriation Act providing the funds expended on it, and (*b*) statutory limits on departmental activity may

Its power to incur liabilities being less strictly dependent upon appropriations and statutory sanction than that of the American executive, the British executive has a wider freedom of manœuvre which may greatly facilitate making policy and inaugurating new pro-

be overridden by an appropriation for an activity otherwise beyond the department's powers. (*Epitome*, p. 725; PAC 1932, Evidence, Q. 840.) The Treasury has admitted, however, that from the point of view of constitutional propriety such cases should be exceptional and that in particular an Appropriation Act should be used to override a statute only in an emergency, constitutional propriety requiring that legislation regularizing the situation be enacted at the earliest possible date, unless the activity is a non-continuing one. (*Epitome*, p. 725, Treasury Minute of 1932.)

The Treasury's argument that an Appropriation Act may authorize an activity and expenditure on it does not explicitly answer the question whether in such cases a department may incur liabilities before the Appropriation has been voted, although the implication would seem to be that it could. Nor does the argument deal with the possibility that just as the power of the Crown includes the power to conduct foreign relations and make treaties without statutory sanction, so also it may, in some instances, include the power to provide services and so incur liabilities without statutory sanction. This raises the question of the limits of the prerogative, whose bounds are notoriously hard to define. It does indeed seem to be some such power to which the Treasury representative referred in an interesting passage at arms with the Comptroller and Auditor General before the PAC in 1932. While granting that 'constitutional principle' required that the Executive must not so commit Parliament to future expenditure as, in effect, to force it to appropriate funds in the future for services without statutory sanction, the Treasury representative insisted that an exception to that principle is 'the law that the King's Government must be carried on', which he took to mean not only that the fighting services might incur liabilities for services without statutory sanction, but also that to some undefined extent the same power was held by the executive in providing civil services (Q. 841).

grammes. An illustration will help bring out some of the possibilities. In the spring of 1953 the Colonial Office, in view of the serious world rice shortage, decided that additional funds should be made available for rice production in the colonies. Legislation authorizing such programmes of development and welfare had been passed between 1940 and 1950, the various Acts authorizing expenditure not to exceed £140 million within a period coming to an end in March 1956. Nearly the whole of this sum had been committed, however, and to attempt to bring the new schemes under the authority so given would probably have meant displacing other developments. To introduce into Parliament new authorizing legislation and a supplementary estimate might have caused delay while the legislation was being prepared and surely would have disrupted the existing parliamentary time-table.

With the concurrence of the Treasury the Colonial Secretary, therefore, instructed colonial governments that they might make commitments for the special rice programme, although his action meant that total commitments would almost certainly rise above the authorized figure of £140 million. He informed the House of Commons of what he had done, announcing at the same time that legislation to authorize the additional expenditure would be introduced early in the next session. The fact of interest to us is that commitments were to be made, not only before an appropriation had been voted but also in contravention of the limit on such expenditure set by Parliament. 'I can see no other way of ensuring that the continuity of colonial development is not interrupted', concluded the Colonial Secretary, 'and I feel confident that I have the full support of the House in the action I am now taking.'[1]

The wider powers of the British as compared with the American executive are particularly marked in the sphere of defence. Possessing them the Government was able, for instance, after the outbreak of the Korean war, to embark upon an increased defence programme covering the ensuing three years, depending on parliamentary legislation only for such appropriations as it thought would be needed to cover expenditures in each financial year. In this instance also, of course, ministers respected the constitutional convention which obliges them to bring new programmes and policies to the attention of Parliament. In consequence there were in the autumn of 1950 several statements in Parliament relating to increases in the defence effort, and in February 1951 a Command Paper sketching the new programme was presented to the House of Commons by ministers, who explained and defended their plans in a two-day debate.[2]

The financial powers of the British executive are wide; considered in themselves, they might be thought to be dangerous. The principal safeguard is, of course, the

---

[1] 516 H.C. Deb. 1898 (24 June 1953).
[2] See footnote, p. 32 above.

convention which obliges ministers continually to explain to Parliament what they are doing and what they propose to do and which permits them to retain their power only so long as they can keep the confidence of the House of Commons. Another and not the least important safeguard is provided by Treasury control. Enjoying great freedom of manœuvre, the executive can, if it chooses, embark on a long-range programme before detailed estimates of the ultimate costs of its constituent parts are feasible or, for that matter, even before a firm idea of the total cost can be framed. This greater liberty to move rapidly and with large measures is also the opportunity to act thoughtlessly, incoherently, and with extravagance. To meet the consequent need for co-ordination and control, the powers of the Treasury have been shaped. Not only will the Treasury authorize expenditure in anticipation of Parliamentary sanction only if the need is urgent, but also through its day-to-day contact with departments it is able to foresee the future implications of their current policy-making. Supply is concerned not simply with expenditure that will fall in any current year, but with any prospective expenditure and any departmental proposal that may at some time in the future lead to expenditure. Its normal powers, therefore, introduce it as of right in the early stages of planning and programming, well before commitments are made or liabilities incurred.

The powers of the Treasury entail consequences of no

little importance in the process of policy-making. Its power to approve future expenditure and the department's need for approval even of an activity that has only contingent financial implications mean that both Treasury and departmental officials will be compelled continually to give thought to the future consequences of their plans and, where policy may be involved, to bring these consequences to the attention of ministers. The future is a matter about which politicians, because of the nature of their situation, have little time to think. By reason of its scope and structure Treasury control tends to induce ministers to look beyond the pressing problems of the moment and, at the same time, provides them with the staff assistance to do so intelligently.

Treasury control and economy

To regard Treasury control as merely a means of cutting costs and saving money is to overlook some of its most important functions in British government. Economy, nevertheless, remains an important purpose of Treasury control and we may usefully conclude this description of the classic form of Treasury control by examining how it is used to enforce economy and how it is related to other machinery serving the same purpose. No doubt, as the Public Accounts Committee has observed, the broadening of the functions of the Treasury in recent years has meant that it directs relatively less of its attention to ensuring economy and efficiency in departmental spending. 'The question that presents it-self', asked the Committee, 'is whether this development has been allowed to go too far.'[1]

Day-to-day control provides a principal opportunity for preventing extravagance. So also does the annual review of the estimates, at which time Supply officials are much concerned 'to squeeze the water out of the sponge'. Estimates cannot be effectively criticized in Parliament, since once the Government has presented them it cannot without loss of face withdraw or alter them as a result of parliamentary pressure. It follows that after estimates have been reviewed and forwarded by departments, the only place where they can be effec-tively criticized from the viewpoint of prudent house-keeping is in the Supply divisions. Some expenditure offers only limited scope for economizing—for instance, a pension or family allowance scheme under which the rates of payment are fixed by statute. Other expenditure may have been recently examined under the heading of proposed new services. But over a great mass of recur-rent expenditure large and small—for instance, expen-ditures on the repair of roads or on the construction of public works—Supply makes this review a principal means of economizing.

How effective is that criticism? Without trying to give a precisely graded answer to this question, we may con-sider here the various safeguards against extravagance

[1] 4th Report, PAC, 1950–1, p. 8.

which operate within the Treasury and outside it. That Treasury officials are very much aware of their responsibility for prudent housekeeping we may be sure. Whether they succeed in this task as well as they might is a question on which opinion is not at one.[1] Critics recall, for example, that in Palmerston's day the Treasury stopped a small war by refusing to agree to the required expenditure,[2] and ask rhetorically whether one could imagine that happening today. Champions of the Treasury point out that, as of old, departments still complain of a too meticulous and detailed control, regarding the Treasury, in words sometimes attributed to Sir Winston Churchill, as 'inverted Micawbers'—that is, 'always waiting for something to turn down'. Still no one would deny that the immense growth of government expenditure has meant that control is much less detailed than it was even a generation ago. If today the Treasury were to try to exercise that degree of detailed control, it is a fair guess that the business of government would come to a grinding halt.

An American will note also that as compared with the massed ranks of accountants, statisticians, and professional budget examiners in the Bureau of the Budget,

---

[1] The PAC, while 'impressed by the keen interest shown by senior officers of the Treasury' in the problems of economy and efficiency, were 'not sure that Treasury control is, as that Department claims, more effective than it was thirty years ago'. 4th Report, 1950–1, p. 8.

[2] C. K. Webster, *The Foreign Policy of Palmerston* (London, 1951), pp. 388–9.

the officials of Supply divisions seem amateur and few. Amateur they are in the sense that most of them are members of the Administrative Class, lacking specialized training in economics, accountancy, public administration, and similar subjects and looking forward to a career which may well take them into other departments. Faithful to the orthodoxy of the British Civil Service, they hold, however, that preferable to expert knowledge is their varied experience in government. And they will point out that from their continuing day-to-day control they quickly gain an intimate acquaintance with departments and officials.

Against the fact that they may seem few in number must be set the arrangements for enforcing economy which have been established within departments. By a major reform of the interwar years, the Permanent Secretary of each department was made also its Accounting Officer. As a result, it is he who answers for the department before the Public Accounts Committee and on him, at the official level, rests the undivided responsibility for both policy and the financial consequence of policy. Over the first stage in the expenditure of public moneys—the formulation of a proposal and the granting of financial authority—the Treasury retains its former control. Similarly, the final or audit stage which is presided over by the Public Accounts Committee remains much the same. With regard to the intervening stage, administration and execution, the Treasury continues to exercise its strict Establishments control and keeps in touch with the progress of expenditure by such means as periodic formal reports on major projects.[1] In other respects, however, it expects the departments themselves, in the persons of their Accounting Officers, to take primary responsibility for their financial administration. In such departmental controls economy is provided with a line of defence outside the Treasury.

Beyond the machinery of housekeeping control by departmental and Supply officials lie other formidable barriers to extravagance. Of these the principal is the annual audit of appropriation accounts, which, although performed in the name of the House of Commons, is also so tied in with the Treasury as to bolster its house-keeping control. In charge of the audit is the Comptroller and Auditor General, an official who is independent of the executive, holding office during good behaviour and being removable only by resolutions of both Houses. As Comptroller he will grant the Treasury credit on the Consolidated Fund only in the amount of the sum total authorized for issue by Parliament—normally in the Consolidated Fund and Appropriation Acts. Unlike the American Comptroller General, however, he does not possess the power of making final settlement or adjustment of claims, nor the power to make advance decisions governing the settlement of accounts.

His principal function is, of course, not control but

[1] See 4th Report, PAC, 1950–1, p. 4.

audit. Under the Act of 1866, on behalf of the House of Commons, he examines departmental accounts in order to determine whether the payments charged to the grants of Parliament are supported by proofs of payment, and whether the money expended has been applied to the purposes for which such grants are intended. By instruction of the Treasury, however, which under the same Act has the power to prescribe the manner in which accounts shall be kept, departments account for their expenditure according to not only the Votes, but also the subheads, of their estimates. To incur expenditure in excess of a subhead is therefore illegal, unless, of course, Treasury sanction of virement has been obtained.

The Comptroller and Auditor General, however, looks not only for any legal irregularity but also for evidence of inefficiency and extravagance—so long as a question of government policy is not raised—and in the normal course it is with criticism of this kind that his reports are mainly concerned. These reports go to the Public Accounts Committee of the House of Commons,[1] the more important points ordinarily being embodied in the Committee's reports to the House.

While the Committee's reports, like the auditors' reports of the U.S. Comptroller General, receive very

---

[1] On the Public Accounts Committee and the Select Committee on Estimates, see Basil Chubb, *The Control of Public Expenditure: financial committees of the House of Commons* (Oxford, 1952).

little attention from the legislature, this does not mean that the work of the Comptroller and Auditor General is without consequence on the management of departments. An established procedure links the results of his work with that of the Treasury, which in this way, although it has not itself conducted the expert housekeeping inquiries of the auditors, is enabled by their findings to make a more effective use of its powers. Centring its inquiries largely on questions raised by the report of the Comptroller and Auditor General and in his presence, the Committee, during its annual examination of the appropriation accounts, summons before it and examines the Accounting Officers of the departments. Present also at this inquiry is a Treasury representative, and upon the comments of the Committee's report the Treasury bases communications giving warning and instruction to departments. It is also the Treasury which replies to the Committee's reports, framing a minute with the help of replies received from the departments concerned. Sometimes, but not often, the Treasury is itself criticized by the Comptroller and Auditor General and is called to book by the Committee. In general the three—Treasury, Comptroller and Auditor General, and Committee on Public Accounts—work together with little friction.

Economy and efficiency are also the concern of the Select Committee on Estimates which after a record of only modest achievement in earlier years has recently earned a very considerable reputation. Appointed to examine estimates and suggest economies, the Committee has interpreted its terms of reference to empower it to make a selective review of government activity with particular emphasis on administrative management— 'organization and methods' is the British equivalent. Like the Accounts Committee, it has the power 'to send for persons, papers and records' and has summoned before it not only departmental officials but also witnesses who are not civil servants. A larger committee than the fifteen-man Accounts Committee, it distributes its thirty-six members among a series of sub-committees which conduct particular inquiries. While it has the assistance of committee clerks and of civil servants appointed by departments to act as liaison officers, these do not provide it with a staff comparable to the large, full-time and, perhaps one should also say, aggressive staffs of Congressional committees. There is, it is true, just a touch of the American investigating committee about it—this was even more true of the powerful Committee on National Expenditure during the war. The similarity, however, must remain distant, since the British committee by its terms of reference, as well as the nature of ministerial responsibility, is precluded from raising questions of policy. Nevertheless, its reports —which have dealt with such questions as the organization and financial affairs of the B.B.C., the work of the Control Commissions in Germany and Austria, the ad-

WORKING MEN'S
COLLEGE
LIBRARY

ministration of development areas, the use of motor fuel oil by government departments, and what has been called its most useful report, organization and methods and its effect on the staffing of government departments—have won praise and attention, even to the extent of being referred to during debates in the House of Commons. Recently it reached a new level of prominence when one of its reports was responsible for a minor, but substantial, clash between the Opposition and the Government.[1] The link between the Committee's work and Treasury control consists in the fact, that while the departments concerned in the individual reports send their replies detailing what consequential action they have taken, the Treasury replies to reports of a general character and co-ordinates departmental reports in order to secure reasonable uniformity of procedure.

This survey of procedures designed to secure prudent housekeeping indicates the great reliance placed upon internal departmental checks. As in Establishments control, there has been in the relations of Supply and departments, 'a trend away from meticulous control of detail in favour of greater delegation to Departments, combined with the use of methods which will enable the Treasury to satisfy itself that the standards of prudent housekeeping are being observed'.[2]

---

[1] 517 H.C. Deb. 419 ff. (1 July 1953). Debate on motion to approve the 8th Report of the Select Committee on Estimates, 1952–3.

[2] Sir Edward Bridges, *Treasury Control*, p. 27.

Yet there are important reasons why, in spite of the broadening of the functions of the Treasury, economy remains a principal object of Treasury control. Certain policies may raise it to a position of special prominence, as when in recent years 'economy drives' have served a policy of disinflation. Quite apart from such implications of policy, the idea of co-ordination itself implies economy. To seek balance in programmes of expenditure involves criticism of extravagance and waste. And while, strictly speaking, such criticism does not concern the total amount of expenditure, that problem also is raised when taxation and the needs of economic life as a whole are considered. To co-ordinate such matters—in the light of the values provided by Government policy—will normally involve economy. If, for instance, a smaller total of expenditure would lead to a greater sum of public good, then that total is extravagant and economizing is in order. Admittedly, such a judgement depends upon large ideas of policy defining wherein lies the public good. Without such ideas economy is meaningless. Instructed by them, 'the traditional co-ordinating department' is bound to make economy a central concern.

III

THE CO-ORDINATION OF
ECONOMIC POLICY

SINCE the interwar years the Treasury, as well as all
major British parties, has absorbed the Keynesian revolution. Like the main body of British economists, officials of the Treasury, while they may differ over the
application of the basic Keynesian propositions, accept
those propositions and the responsibility of the Government 'to use fiscal measures to hold the balance between
the money in people's pockets and what they [can] buy
with it'. Since the appearance of the first National
Income White Paper in 1941 and Kingsley-Wood's
Budget Speech of that year, the 'inflationary-deflationary
scheme' in making the Budget has become 'a well-
established and important feature of the aims of Treasury control'.[1]

British Governments, however, whether Labour or
Conservative, have accepted responsibilities wider than
those of restraining inflation and maintaining employment. They will use the powers of government for the
sake not only of economic equilibrium but also of
economic progress, and to promote productivity by

[1] Sir Edward Bridges, *Treasury Control*, p. 18.

investment in the nationalized industries, by tax policy, and by other means has become one of their main concerns. Likewise, the problem of the balance of payments, while not entirely new, has been so much more urgent since the war as to absorb a great deal of the attention of any Government. One might also add that Conservative as well as Labour Governments have sought— as agreed by all parties in the war-time Coalition— 'to secure the production and equitable distribution of essential supplies',[1] although, of course, over what distribution is 'equitable' and what means will be effective, parties may greatly differ.

Models of co-ordination

From the acceptance by parties and Governments of these wider responsibilities, it does not necessarily follow that the Treasury shall be the centre of co-ordination of economic policy. There are two plausible reasons why it ought to be. Since the other parts of the Treasury are concerned with expenditure, taxation, and similar items of financial policy, it would seem to make sense to put the co-ordination of economic policy, which involves these matters at so many points, in the same agency. Furthermore, the Treasury is the only department that is in regular contact with every other department of government from the Ministry of Defence to the Depart-

[1] Herbert Morrison, *Government and Parliament* (London, 1954), p. 288.

ment of Health for Scotland and co-ordination has long been of the essence of its control of financial policy.

But the question is not simple. May not economic policy depend as much for its success upon matters which are the concern of other departments—for instance, the supply of raw materials or of manpower? And in general is it not a little odd that so Gladstonian an institution as the Treasury should become the agency for guiding and controlling state intervention in the economy? Other solutions than the Treasury one are conceivable. Indeed, in reviewing public discussion and administrative practice over the past thirty years or so, it is striking how many different solutions to the problem of economic co-ordination have been proposed and how long it has taken for the present Treasury system to be worked out and adopted. Discussion goes back at least to the report of the Haldane Committee in 1918. From its cautious suggestions could be drawn support for the view that a group of experts without departmental posts be set up as an Economic General Staff working under a non-departmental minister in general charge of economic planning and co-ordination.[1] In its pure form this 'model' could meet with little approval, but there was a strong trace of it in the Ministry of Production which

[1] In the Postscript to his *Full Employment in a Free Society* (New York, 1945), Lord Beveridge advocated an Economic General Staff. For a telling criticism of this idea, see Sir John Anderson, *The Organization of Economic Studies in Relation to the Problems of Government* (London, 1947).

was set up in 1942 to co-ordinate and direct the agencies dealing more closely with war production.

Another possibility is suggested by the organization for defence. The old Committee of Imperial Defence was for long one of the more successful pieces of government machinery. The conscious attempt to follow this precedent in setting up the Economic Advisory Council in 1930 was a failure.[1] The war-time organization on the military side, however, has claimed serious consideration as a model. At the ministerial level, the Defence Committee, over which Churchill presided, dealt with the main lines of production programmes as well as the military plans of the Chiefs of Staff Committee and the joint staffs. At the official level the Chiefs of Staff Committee stood at the head of an elaborate system of joint staff planning, manned by persons drawn from the fighting services and civil departments. By means of this machinery plans were worked out and decided on, the Chiefs of Staff Committee having the executive authority to issue to commanders-in-chief unified operational instructions and strategical guidance on the conduct of the war, leaving only the responsibility for routine administration to the service departments, which followed up the central directives with detailed instructions to their respective commanders-in-chief.[2] How this system might

---

[1] Sir John Anderson, *The Organization of Economic Studies*, pp. 10 ff.

[2] Cmd. 6923, *Central Organization for Defence* (1946).

be adapted to the organization of central economic planning has been sketched by H. R. G. Greaves.[1]

Quite different from these two 'centralist' possibilities, as well as from the present arrangement, was the machinery actually used in the first years of the post-war Labour Government. Its model and predecessor was the Lord President's Co-ordinating Committee for Home Affairs, which, assisted by the newly created Economic Section of the Cabinet Office and Central Statistical Office, had exercised during the war large powers of economic co-ordination on the home front and which no less an authority than Sir John Anderson had pronounced 'a satisfactory type of organization . . . at last evolved, after trial and experiment extending over more than twenty years'.[2] After the war this large ministerial committee, similarly assisted and under its non-departmental minister, supervised the whole field of home and economic affairs, the export drive, however, being directed by the Board of Trade and fiscal policy being left in the hands of the Treasury. At the official level, while the Economic Section and Central Statistical Office were retained, joint staff planning, such as the Joint War Production Staff of the Ministry of Production had attempted, was abandoned, and for co-ordination the Government depended upon the familiar device of interdepartmental committees whose work was super-

[1] H. R. G. Greaves, *The Civil Service in the Changing State*, ch. vii.
[2] *The Organization of Economic Studies*, p. 16.

vised by a committee of the permanent heads of the main economic departments. This committee was the 'central economic team' responsible for gathering data, preparing forecasts, advising ministers, and framing plans and supervising their execution.[1] It was assisted by interdepartmental committees or working parties concerned with such problems as manpower, capital investment, raw materials, and the balance of payments.

The crises of 1947 revealed the weaknesses of this arrangement. No doubt the primary responsibility for the crises should be laid on the far too expansive policy of the Government. Neither ministers, nor officials, nor for that matter the public, fully realized in the first post-war years how serious were the economic problems facing Britain, and the shock of events in 1947, in particular the fuel crisis of February and the convertibility crisis of August, did much to create a new atmosphere favourable to hard decisions and vigorous measures. The spectacle of the rapid melting away of the American loan, for instance, could not but have a sobering effect upon departmental claims for dollars.

But the machinery was also to blame. There was need not only for a new spirit of sober realism but also for more centralized authority. One fault was the division of responsibility for economic affairs among the Lord President, the Board of Trade, and the Treasury. 'Until

[1] Herbert Morrison, 'Economic Planning', *Public Administration* (Spring, 1947), p. 30.

economic planning was absorbed into the Treasury organization,' Mr. Morrison has remarked, 'it was a matter of some doubt how far the Treasury was subject to the machinery of economic co-ordination.'[1] The members of the supervising committee of permanent heads, being heavily burdened with departmental duties, were hard put to find time properly to prepare and follow up decisions, and in general the system of interdepartmental committees tended to diffuse responsibility and to encourage compromise among departmental claims rather than firm decisions based on a consistent line of policy. As D. N. Chester has concluded, the experience of the years 1945–7 showed that something stronger than 'the normal interdepartmental machinery of co-ordination' was necessary if 'a clear national economic policy' was to be decided on and put across.[2]

From the crises of 1947 the Treasury emerged as the centre of economic planning and co-ordination. As the review of other 'models' has suggested, there were, however, other alternatives. Conceivably, the old machinery might have been continued. More interesting speculations are suggested by the possibility of a 'centralist' solution. Suppose, for instance, that the Government had chosen to revert to war-time methods of quantitative planning and physical control. These methods, of course,

[1] *Government and Parliament*, p. 308.
[2] G. D. N. Worswick and P. H. Ady (eds.), *The British Economy 1945–50* (Oxford, 1952), p. 363.

greatly reduce the importance of finance. During the war the main economic decisions were made in the course of determining such matters as a man-power budget which stated how the total labour force was to be allocated among the chief industries and the fighting services; budgets for critical materials indicating how they were to be used within the economy; an import programme which set out the physical volume, as well as the cost, of various types of imports for a certain period. The use of such quantitative programmes for production has been called the outstanding feature of British war-time economic organization[1] and in 1947, especially, but not exclusively, among those inclining to the Left-wing of the Labour Party, many believed that they should be the heart of central economic planning in peace-time as well.

As during the war the decline of finance had greatly reduced the Treasury's role as co-ordinator—for much of the time the Chancellor of the Exchequer was not in the War Cabinet—so the revival of war-time planning methods would have called for a system of co-ordination quite different from the one actually adopted. If the model of defence organization had been followed, there would have been, on the official plane, a system of joint staff planning. Joint staffs drawn from departments, but with executive authority, would have decided on the

---

[1] Hubert Henderson, *The Uses and Abuses of Economic Planning* (Cambridge, 1947), p. 10.

main economic objectives and worked out in more or less detail quantitative programmes for achieving them —some equivalent of 'unified operational instructions'. The role of departments would have been to carry these programmes into execution, and in the relationship of planners and departments there would have been something of the military relation of command and obedience. The task of this central organization would have been not merely co-ordination but positive direction.

Even less interdepartmental would have been a variant of Max Weber's model of 'monocratic bureaucracy'. In such a scheme each person (or department) has a clearly delimited area of responsibility which he administers with powers of command. As those below him are subject to his command, so is he subject to the orders of his superiors. Each area of responsibility is part of a logical pattern determined by higher authority. At the peak of the hierarchy designed in accord with this model stands a single person, a 'super-minister', assisted by his non-departmental staff, which prepares the elaborate system of plans and orders to be executed under his unifying authority.

Such possibilities are not fanciful when one considers the tasks which may arise in economic planning. For example, to curtail the supply of some critical material will have important repercussions throughout the economy. To foresee these would take vast knowledge and to anticipate them an elaborate system of decision-making and control. Above all, if the shape of the economy, of its future structure as well as its present operations of production and distribution, are to be controlled by governmental decisions, a single centre with the power to direct and command in accord with a unified and consistent system of plans may well seem indispensable. Conceivably, modern econometrics and calculating machines put it within the power of governments to assemble the information and make the great network of decisions which such an approach would entail.

These speculations may suggest extremes which were not real alternatives in 1947. Nevertheless, the acute economic problems of the time—shortages of critical materials, strong inflationary pressures, a growing deficit in the balance of payments—made some sort of 'centralist' solution plausible. To understand why such a solution was not adopted would take us well beyond the scope of the present inquiry and would mean examining forces in British public opinion and the British economy as well as British government. Certainly the difficulties of getting the public—labour and consumers as well as industry—to accept war-time methods of command and central direction were important considerations. Rather similar obstacles arising from the nature of British government and administration also affected the outcome. 'Cabinet democracy'—the phrase is Mr. Morrison's—means that no single minister can be given final, overriding authority over others responsible for departments. It follows that a 'super-minister' in charge of economic affairs would not in fact be able to frame economic plans without regard for departmental pressures and demands. Compromise would certainly disrupt any machine-made, econometrically perfect scheme that he might produce. Similarly, the relation of command and obedience is foreign to the habits and spirit of the Civil Service, particularly the members of the Administrative Class, when one department is dealing with another. Between officials of different departments the relations are rather those of what Professor Austin Robinson has called 'Civil Service democracy'. No more than ministers do departments—not even the Treasury—order one another about. Great as may be the authority of the Treasury, its officials in actual practice work not by command but by consultation, persuasion, and not infrequently concession. The Treasury 'style' of co-ordination is not the product of unenlightened Gladstonian attitudes in Great George Street. As will appear from our discussion in Chapter IV, it is intimately connected with the spirit and structure of the whole frame of government.

If we examine the role of the Treasury in economic co-ordination, it is in such larger traits—in the style, rather than in particular methods—that we see the likeness between the old and the new Treasury. Unlike the methods of Treasury control over expenditure, these methods cannot be described as a more or less settled system. They have varied greatly, being adapted with more or less success to changing circumstances—changes in the rate of rearmament, in the degree of inflationary pressures, in the terms of trade. Nor does one often find precise parallels between the methods of the old and new Treasury. Without stretching the point, one might at certain times have found real similarities between the annual review of estimates of expenditure and the review of investment programmes or of import programmes. On the other hand, while the Treasury has kept in frequent touch with the economic activities of departments, there are no procedures in the realm of economic co-ordination comparable to those flowing from the requirement of prior approval. With regard to such activities, indeed, the Treasury has at no time had that complete control which it traditionally has enjoyed over activities with a financial aspect.

In a broader sense, however, as comparison with other models of co-ordination suggests, the new is essentially like the old. Treasury control, old or new, is not positive direction: that is to say, the Treasury does not itself commonly take the initiative, dictating to departments what they shall undertake in order to fulfil government policy or plans. Rather it shapes the initiative already taken by departments, by a criticism which is mainly negative bringing that initiative into accord with policy. Furthermore, while the Treasury has in some respects powers of command—negative command—in the actual practice of administration, its officials, as well as its ministers, carry out their work mainly by persuasion and compromise, as well as by the exercise of authority. Officials in Economic Affairs, as well as in Supply, work closely with departmental officials. They are not interested parties on the same footing as departmental officials, since they have their broader task of winning acceptance of Government policy. But their task is 'winning acceptance of policy', rather than 'enforcing policy', for they do not in fact have the power of the 'monocratic bureaucrat' or the joint staff. The officials with whom they deal are not subordinates but equals, representing other 'great departments of state' operating under the system of 'Cabinet democracy'.

The resulting process is neither what would occur within a purely interdepartmental committee, nor what would be accomplished by an agency with powers of positive direction. It is adequate to co-ordinate policy and to guide a limited degree of economic planning. Its style, however, fits ill with detailed, quantitative planning, and the adoption of the Treasury solution in 1947 undoubtedly had not a little to do with the movement away from that kind of planning and control which set in long before the Conservatives took office. The forces of 'Cabinet democracy' and 'Civil Service democracy' worked in the same direction as those of British democracy in general.

Machinery of economic planning

On the ministerial level the principal reform of 1947 was to put an end to the division of command in economic affairs by centring authority over them in Sir Stafford Cripps who became Chancellor of the Exchequer. The responsibility for economic co-ordination, which had been briefly vested in the short-lived Ministry of Economic Affairs, now was added to the traditional duties of the Chancellor. Reforms of Cabinet committees included the establishment of the small Economic Policy Committee which consisted of ministers from the chief economic departments and of which the Prime Minister became chairman. To this committee were given the tasks of co-ordinating economic policy at home and abroad which had formerly been vested in the Lord President's Committee and the Overseas Policy Committee.

On the official level there was a similar shift of authority towards the Treasury. While the official committee of heads of the economic departments remained, the function of 'the central economic team' was transferred to a new body, the Central Economic Planning Staff. Briefly located in the Lord President's Office, the CEPS was put under Sir Stafford while he held the office of Minister of Economic Affairs and then followed him to the Treasury where it has remained. When, shortly after the February fuel crisis, Sir Stafford, then acting as Chairman of the Lord President's Committee during Mr. Morrison's illness, first informed the House of the

Government's intention to create this body, he described it as 'a joint planning staff, somewhat on the lines of the procedure that was so successfully developed in the war'.[1] Consisting of departmental planning officers, who would have their own staffs, it was to have a full-time executive head, assisted also by a small, picked staff and secretariat. It also had as industrial consultant during the initial stages the former chief executive at the Ministry of Production, while its head was a business-man who had served in the Ministry of Aircraft Produc-tion during the war. The notion of a joint planning staff for economic affairs, however, did not materialize and what finally appeared in its stead was a relatively small unit in the Treasury. The directors of plans were never appointed, and while members of the staff have been drawn from departments, their work in the CEPS has occupied their full time.

If the CEPS did not become a joint planning staff, what was its function? In numbers it was, and remains, small—hardly more than thirty even when personal assistants and clerical workers are included—the prin-cipal officials, apart from its chief, being four or five Assistant Secretaries and some three Under Secretaries. A Chief Planning Officer was its head until 1953 when the CEPS was put directly under the new deputy to the Permanent Secretary of the Treasury. Nor has the staff been expert in the usual sense, in its first years its mem-

[1] 434 H.C. Deb. 970 (10 Mar. 1947).

bers including only one economist by training. Like the officials of the Supply divisions, they have been rather administrators, usually with varied experience in government. For expert economic advice the CEPS has relied upon the Economic Section of the Cabinet Office, which is manned by professional economists and which in its operations was virtually part of Economic Affairs long before its transfer to the Treasury in 1953. The function of the CEPS was not to give such expert advice but to use it in keeping a watch on the present and future economic consequences of departmental activities. In the CEPS these activities could be continually measured against the economic problems of the country and from it recommendations of how departmental activities ought to be shaped in the light of these larger needs could be obtained. What it did can best be seen if we look at its relations with the interdepartmental committees concerned with economic matters.

In the reorganization of interdepartmental machinery which took place in 1947 no single pattern was followed, and the structure which resulted illustrated the varied nature of the economic problems which had to be faced in that year and for some years afterwards. One of the most pressing of these problems was the shortage of certain critical materials. The interdepartmental organization which had dealt with this question during the war and in the years immediately following was continued after 1947, but its inevitable tendency to reflect specifically departmental interests was corrected to some extent by its having available to it thenceforward the advice of the CEPS. It was therefore able to relate divergencies of departmental interests to the wider background of the needs and resources of the economy as a whole.

By contrast, the problems arising from Marshall Aid and from the consequences of the convertibility crisis were novel, and new machinery had therefore to be devised to deal with them. After the suspension of convertibility in August 1947, the Government moved on to a policy of bilateral trade and financial negotiations. In the circumstances, this meant that there had to be a widely representative body of officials which could meet frequently, handle the flow of telegrams, and have quick access to ministers so that the decisions which were continually required could be given without delay. Moreover, since the negotiations had political and diplomatic aspects, and sometimes involved the interests of the Dominions and Colonies, the new machinery had to provide room for the views not only of the Treasury and the Board of Trade, but also the Foreign Office and the Colonial and Commonwealth Relations Offices. And the Treasury interest itself was not confined to strictly financial questions or to the technique of payments arrangements; it comprised also the contribution which the CEPS could offer by relating, once again, the details of a particular negotiation to the wider context of the policies dictated by the needs of the economy as a whole. It was therefore a natural development which, after a time, found the 'home' for this new piece of interdepartmental machinery in the Economic Affairs side of the Treasury where it came under the general supervision of the Chief Planning Officer.

The arrangements for controlling the investment programme of the country and its import programme are also of interest as illustrating some of the familiar traits of the Treasury style of co-ordination. We may consider them next; and, after looking at the form of Treasury control which they exemplify, we shall turn to the broader phases of economic policy making, emphasizing especially the framing of the Budget, which, after the first expansive years of the Labour Government, became more and more the principal instrument of such economic planning and control as was to be undertaken.

Investment programming

Capital investment in both the public and private sectors of the economy bore directly upon two acute problems of the crisis period—the shortage of critical materials such as steel and timber, and the strong tendencies to inflation—and continued to be central to two long-run problems of the British economy—the need to raise productivity and the need to expand exports. It was therefore necessary to create new machinery to carry out the task of programming capital investment, a type

WORKING MEN'S
COLLEGE
LIBRARY

of quantitative planning which was carried into execution by direct physical controls, especially the building licences. By means of the new machinery, the focal point of which was the CEPS, departmental programmes of investment were examined, the resulting appraisal of the country's investment programme as a whole being forwarded as a recommendation to ministers.

From the start there was a certain resemblance between this new type of programming and the review of financial estimates by the Supply divisions. In October departments were asked for estimates of their investment programmes. The departments concerned would include those which directly made investment, such as the Ministry of Works and the Admiralty, those which presented the claims of nationalized industries, and those which stood in the relation of sponsor to private industry and submitted requirements on its behalf. Since investment takes time to mature and needs to be planned well in advance, the programme as a whole covered a period of three years. It was hoped that the new estimates received in the autumn would need to relate mainly to the third year alone, while the programme for the two years preceding would remain as previously approved. In practice, however, recurrent balance of payments problems, decisions about defence expenditure, materials difficulties, and so on, meant that there often had to be wholesale revisions of many programmes already provisionally approved.

The programming of investment had to be related, of course, to the general condition of the economy and had to have regard to such questions as whether and how far the sum total of investment projected would be inflationary. This meant taking into account economic estimates —for example, forecasts of the course of the balance of payments and of the size of the gross national product and its distribution—being prepared elsewhere within the planning machine. Such estimates were indispensable if the investment programme was to be seen in a proper perspective and the particular problems which it involved were to be thrown into clear relief.

As in their relations with Supply, it was the departments that took the initiative, they, not the planning staff, drawing up and proposing the various projected schemes of investment. Equally the objective of investment programming was not merely to reduce investment as the task of Supply is not merely to cut expenditure. The need to prevent the investment programme from being too inflationary often implied the need to reduce the projected total, and this involved applying the priorities of Government policy in achieving that end. Moreover, in so far as those priorities left open various choices of investment pattern, other factors involving economic and technical criteria had to be taken into account. Yet even in this realm the appraisal could not be merely that of the technician or the economist; continually the problems included an area of indeterminacy which called for

85

the judgement of the administrator. A strength of the expert—the professional economist for example—is that he recognizes the typical problems of his science when he sees them and, unlike the amateur, is not obliged to think out each one anew. A weakness is that he may insist on staying within the premises and logical demands of that science, making different forecasts depending upon different assumptions and refusing to choose between various assumptions until he has 'enough' data. The administrator, however, often cannot wait; he 'lives in time'. It is his task and his 'expertise' to assess the probabilities, often of necessity on other than economic grounds—as when he considers whether or not timber supplies will be forthcoming from a particular source—and come to a decision. That decision will perhaps hedge some of the important choices, and will not, in operation, accord perfectly with actual events. But neither will it be as widely wrong as it might have been if the administrator had acted entirely on one set of assumptions.

It is important to make these observations in order not to exaggerate the degree of economic rationality achieved by the new machinery for the programming of investment. In practice the form of economic co-ordination and control evolved was less schematic and more flexible, less concentrated in one place and more empirical, than if the approach to planning had derived from concepts requiring a high degree of quantitative precision in forecasts and results.

To shape programmes to fit both the inherent ambiguity of events and the political forces that make policy is of the essence of co-ordination, whether in the traditional exercise of balancing the Budget or in the business of economic planning. No machinery which functions at the official level can solve this problem with finality; the ultimate decision must, of course, rest with ministers. But the machinery by which the investment programme of the country as a whole was carefully examined in the light of both Government policy and economic probabilities was of great assistance to ministers in discharging their final responsibility.

Moreover, it proved capable of adapting itself to the new situation which developed as the British economy emerged from the period of acute shortages and inflationary pressure. As the old system of control by building licence was gradually lifted, the Budget became one of the principal means of shaping investment in the private sector, while, as regards the public sector, the issue became one of framing general lines of investment policy rather than of criticizing and limiting the particular programmes submitted by individual departments. In this process the Supply divisions, the Home Finance Division (with its connexions with the banking system and with the capital financing of government activity), the Economic Section, and the CEPS could all co-operate with advantage.

The programming as a whole continued to cover a

period of three years. Annually in the autumn each department concerned with investment forwarded to the Treasury its investment estimates. In the light of these estimates, recommendations could be framed about the level and pattern of investment which would conform most closely with Government policy and the way in which that level or pattern might be achieved. But the procedure was also more closely related to the normal work of financial control. Previously investment programmes were based on calendar years; now, like estimates of expenditure, they were based on financial years, and the forward programming of investment over several years ahead came into line with the forward estimating of expenditure over the same period. In this way the demands of investment and the exigencies of finance were related more closely to each other in that final process of establishing economic policy which emerges in the Budget. And in general, while the control over investment remained much less detailed than the control over expenditure, the result was not only to link the co-ordination of investment more closely with the co-ordination of expenditure, but also to make it, as an administrative process, even more like that familiar form of Treasury control.

Import programming

The task of controlling imports, although it involved very different considerations (above all, of course, the needs of the balance of payments), resembled the task of controlling investment in that it involved decisions which took the form of quantitative programmes which were carried into execution by physical controls—import licensing and foreign exchange control. Here again, the issue was one of scrutinizing the programmes put forward by interested departments—both those directly engaged in importation and those which sponsored importing private industry—and recommending to ministers a total import programme which was consistent with both Government policy and the needs of the economy. The problems involved were inevitably the chief concern of Overseas Finance, though here again the advice of the CEPS was valuable as enabling individual issues to be related to the requirements and capacities of the economy as a whole. And in so far as Overseas Finance supervised the administration of the controls through which, in particular cases, the import programme would be executed—for instance, a purchase of some commodity from abroad by a department—the relation of Overseas Finance to departments was not unlike that of Supply divisions to departments.

The problems created by import programming were as urgent as those involved in the programming of investment, and certainly the pressures were as acute—for instance, the demand of transport for oil; of housing for timber; of consumers for more generous rations. But, like Supply, Overseas Finance tried to carry the interested departments with it in the process of discussion round the table and the objective was to present to ministers a recommendation which had been inter-departmentally agreed. This meant full and often prolonged debate.[1] Sometimes the economic situation required cuts in the current programmes of departments; more often, however, the task was one of holding down further claims. Success could be measured by the extent to which departments could be brought to accept a pattern of programmes which reflected current policy in terms of the reserves, and so far as agreement was not reached at the official level, the report to ministers

---

[1] In his description of how raw materials were allocated during the war, Sir Oliver Franks has given a portrait of the internal working of committees which throws light on the nature of 'Civil Service democracy'. He writes: 'At these . . . tables where the general plans for raw materials were made, decisions were reached after open discussion and argument between those concerned, whether as suppliers or users. Each member of these committees had to make his case in the presence of his rival claimant or claimants. All on each committee had the same statistical information and all claims were subject to ruthless cross-examination by interested parties. This argumentative process was an essential condition of success. No lonely individual, however excellent the scheme of allocation he had worked out, could have presented it with any hope of acceptance to one of these committees. This type of central planning only works if those who are involved in the decision feel bound by it and convinced by rational considerations that what is proposed is as fair and reasonable as can be in the circumstances. A general plan or allocation is not only a theoretical exercise in distributive justice but a practical directive for ensuing action. It is necessary that the principal agents should acknowledge a commitment to the decision.' *Central Planning and Control in War and Peace* (Cambridge, Mass., 1947), p. 12.

would state what claims could not be brought within these limits, and also what would probably be the economic consequences of granting them.

As the economic situation gradually eased, and the scope of direct import control was reduced, the procedure was modified in a way which tended to substitute for the former rigid limits on imports, commodity by commodity, a more flexible system of monetary quotas for non-sterling imports, departments (such as the Ministry of Food and the Ministry of Materials) being given quotas within which they were fairly free to alter the pattern of imports with which they were concerned. While this change lessened the difficulty and urgency of the work involved, the basic principle that the Treasury centralized and focused potentially conflicting departmental interests, and attempted to secure interdepartmental agreement on a certain pattern of import expenditure, remained the same.

On the whole, this machinery achieved a remarkable degree of agreement. Its results may appear to have been rather less economically rational than might have been desired. When imports of raw materials were cut, for instance, it might, theoretically, have been possible to discriminate more precisely between particular materials, giving certain ones a priority exactly proportionate to the need for them in investment and other spheres. But to ask for so high a degree of economic rationality in cases where factors other than the purely economic inevitably affect the final decision, is probably to expect more than any administrative machine can possibly achieve.

What can the outside observer learn from the experience of these years? D. N. Chester is right in saying that the events of 1945–7 showed that something stronger than the usual interdepartmental machinery was necessary.[1] That British government could provide such stronger machinery was proved by the experience of the three or four succeeding years. Yet certain of the limits which that system of government and administration set upon the machinery of co-ordination were also revealed. On the one hand, economic rationality would seem to demand that authority be firmly centralized in order that the various claims to be considered may be subjected to a clear and coherent decision. Undoubtedly some degree of centralization is not only necessary but also feasible. Yet at some point such centralization tends to become self-defeating. Excellent as a programme or decision may be in the light of economic canons, it loses its value so far as it fails to be acceptable to those who must carry it out. 'It is necessary', as Sir Oliver Franks has said, 'that the principal agents should acknowledge a commitment to the decision.'[2]

In the British system with its plural executive standing at the head of separate departments, commitment can be ensured only if departments and members of the execu-

---

[1] Above, p. 72.   [2] Above, p. 90, n. 1.

tive are brought into and given a full role in the making of relevant decisions. If such participation and commitment are sacrificed for the sake of what may seem to be economic rationality, execution will lose in effectiveness. A certain balance, in short, needs to be found between an excessive departmentalism which impairs the coherence of decisions and an excessive centralization which hampers execution. Such a balance has been worked out over the generations in the classic form of Treasury control. From the midst of continual adjustments, this form in general outline has tended to reappear in the relations of the Treasury and departments in the new field of economic co-ordination.

Phases of policy-making

Since 1947, if not before, the principal instrument of economic planning and control has been the Budget, the shift of authority to the Treasury and the movement away from physical controls having greatly enhanced its importance. Primarily it has been a means of restraining inflation, and Chancellors of both parties have annually sought to achieve a substantial surplus. Budgetary policy, however, has also been guided by other purposes than that of maintaining general economic equilibrium. The encouragement of export industries and the raising of productivity are obvious examples. As these examples suggest, the Budget can also provide the opportunity for applying not only general fiscal controls—such as heavy taxation of incomes in order to restrain inflation—but also more particular controls —such as taxes on certain products in order to discourage their sale on the home market, or allowances to encourage investment. The controls, general or particular, provided by the Budget need to be made to work in harmony with the other means by which the Government may choose to affect the economy. These have included, as in the cases of capital investment and imports, direct physical controls used to execute quantitative programmes. Equally important are other means, such as subsidies of various types; manipulation of the interest rate; measures to affect credit policy; direct government investment and government guarantees to encourage certain types of investment. Indeed, the whole field of government expenditure, current and capital, provides a great variety of controls, general or particular, which may be used and must be co-ordinated.

So complicated a problem might seem to call for a high degree of system: a system of thought, such as that provided by the 'input-output' approach to economic analysis, which would enable planners to evaluate accurately all factors in the economy and the bearing of government activity upon them;[1] and a system of procedure in administration which would ensure that the vast multitude of government decisions would actually

---

[1] See Wassily Leontief, 'Econometrics', in *A Survey of Contemporary Economics*, Howard S. Ellis (ed.) (Philadelphia, 1948), p. 407.

be guided by the conclusions of such analysis. System in this sense and in such a degree will not be found in British administration, the reason and justification being much the same as those which rule out the possibility of comprehensive quantitative planning under strongly centralized authority. In the business of economic co-ordination there are, however, certain elements of system, both in the way people think about economic problems and in the way they go about making decisions, which facilitate the task.

A theoretical framework in terms of which many, though not all, Britain's economic problems can be approached is provided by the familiar Keynesian equations: $Y = C + I$ and $S = I$. The economist will find nothing astonishing in this; he is continually advising governments that these are premises from which economic policy should proceed. The political scientist may, however, be a little amazed to find a government sufficiently sensitive to theory to take really in earnest these propositions and the system of which they are a part, applying them in the framing of policy, following them in the making of decisions. It is a fact that in the Treasury, among both ministers and officials, the Keynesian system to at least a commonsense level of sophistication has been worked into the grain of thought and administration. This means that they share a common way of thinking about economic problems, not the least advantage of which is that administrators can understand and sympathize with the advice they receive from professional economists.

One set of critical estimates and decisions follows from the national income forecasts which are periodically prepared by a group of economists and statisticians. Their principal problem is to arrive at an estimate of the annual gross national product for the next few years. Once this estimate has been made, they can indicate various ways in which the national product might be divided up among the four principal factors constituting the right-hand side of the $Y = C + I$ equation—government current expenditure, personal consumption, gross investment, and the foreign balance—basing their forecasts upon existing policy or upon ministerial instructions as to possible changes in policy. With the aid of such a report, ministers, assisted by the appropriate official advice, will make final decisions. These forecasts, for instance, would be used by the Chancellor, when with his senior advisers he considers the recommendations which have resulted from the investment programming exercise and decides on the desirable course of investment in public and private sectors.

The task of the Budget in the inflationary-deflationary scheme is sharply defined by the problem of balancing savings and investment. The outlines of this problem are given by the combined capital account of public and private units which is regularly published as a part of the *Economic Survey*. The central question is how to ensure that there shall be set aside from national income sums sufficient to finance investment—that is, gross domestic investment set against the positive or negative foreign balance. Personal saving is notoriously hard to estimate and hard also to control or even affect with any degree of precision. More manageable is the figure for company savings; the distributed profits tax, for example, can encourage or discourage it with roughly calculable effect. In bridging the inflationary gap, the principal means, of course, is the surplus of the central government and local authorities on current account. In particular the surplus for which the Chancellor must budget to avoid excessive inflation and for which he can budget without too greatly adverse effects in other respects—for example, on incentives—is a critical question.

None of these decisions, whether relating to the general health of the economy or the more particular problems, can be made in isolation. Economic necessity requires that each be co-ordinated as closely as possible with the others. The method is that of successive approximations, each decision being made first in the light of a tentative forecast of the others, then revised as these forecasts and decisions become firmer. Without meaning to exaggerate the degree of system involved, one may say that this process is concentrated mainly in the period between the early autumn and the early part of the New Year and is roughly divided into four phases. In the first three, emphasis falls successively upon problems principally related to the investment programme, the balance of payments, and the forecast of national income, while in the fourth the main question is the final shape of the Budget.

One product of the first three phases is the *Economic Survey* which, covering the calendar, not the financial year, is published some time before the Chancellor opens his Budget. The first draft, for which the CEPS blocks out the form, is made by the Economic Section and then goes back to the CEPS for revision; thence it makes a circuitous journey through the committee of permanent heads of the economic departments and through other bodies to ministers. While the *Survey*, particularly in recent years, has paid more attention to the past than to the future, it usually falls into three main parts, which reflect the major phases in the process of policy-making. It will commonly contain forecasts—the word 'target' which figured largely in the first *Surveys* has been dropped for the more modest term—and statements of policy for the coming year or years, as in 1951 on the urgency of the new defence programme or in 1952 on the 'immediate task ahead' of bringing the sterling area back into balance with the outside world. These forecasts and statements will reflect programmes, such as that for investment, and while the *Survey* will, of course, not indicate what the Budget will be, its forecasts being based on existing rates of taxation and fiscal policy, it will probably point up the problems the Budget will have to deal with and from it observers can make their own guesses—sometimes fairly accurate guesses—of the outlines of new fiscal policy.

The *Survey*, then, is certainly not an operational plan. Yet it introduces an element of system into the framing of plans and policies and in the field of economic policy performs something of the function of the estimates and their review in the sphere of expenditure. When published it gives Parliament and the public a notion of the general outlines of policy and programmes. And in its preparation it helps, and indeed obliges, officials and ministers concerned with economic co-ordination to look at economic policy as a whole, bringing out inconsistencies, overlapping, and long-run consequences which might otherwise be overlooked.

Framing the Budget

The fourth phase is framing the Budget. In British usage this term refers to the Chancellor's proposals for taxation, and on Budget Day the business formally before the House is the set of resolutions relating to taxation and borrowing. Obviously, when the Chancellor explains his revenue proposals to the House, as when he has previously worked out their formulation, he must consider expenditure and economic policy as well as revenue. In British constitutional practice the Budget is the Chancellor's responsibility. Yet even in the narrower sense of merely the revenue proposals, the Budget directly and indirectly affects all departments and the

WORKING MEN'S
COLLEGE
LIBRARY

whole of Government policy and therefore, it would seem, is a matter that would need to be previously discussed at length not only by ministers but also by officials against the background of thorough staff preparation. This has not, however, been the traditional practice. Before the war as a rule the recommendations were drawn up by a few Treasury officials, who could at that time do practically the whole job. Even today revenue proposals, singly or as a whole, are not discussed by interdepartmental committees and indeed the Cabinet itself is normally informed of the content of the Budget as a whole only a short time—perhaps only a few hours —before the Chancellor presents it to the House. It has been said among M.P.s that even so important a measure as the 'once and for all' capital levy of 1950 was discussed by the Chancellor with only a few advisers before being revealed to the Cabinet as part of the Budget at a meeting on the day before he presented the Budget to the House. That same secrecy with which the Budget is guarded from the public eye before Budget Day has traditionally prevailed in almost equal degree within the bureaucracy and even the Government itself.

The reason given for this procedure is much the same in each case: tax proposals must be kept secret in order to prevent forestalling. The argument may seem a little thin, even as a defence of preventing public and parliamentary discussion of tax proposals before they are voted as law. But as applied to the administration it must

seem highly implausible in the eyes of the outside observer. For one thing, many matters are nowadays discussed by interdepartmental committees that could be
exploited for profit by an unscrupulous civil servant with
equal or even greater effect. What is far more important,
however, is the gap which this procedure would leave in
the machinery of co-ordination, if it were not qualified in
practice.

The fact of the matter seems to be that, while the old
convention is still upheld in formal procedures, in actual
practice the framing of the Budget takes account of the
wider implications of the process of economic analysis
and planning which have emerged from the discussions
of previous months; and although knowledge of the
Budget proposals in their entirety is confined to a few
of the Chancellor's most senior advisers, there will be a
great deal of consultation with experts and department
officials on particular aspects of these proposals.

At the time the Budget is being framed, or in a discussion of some economic problem during the year, an
official may indeed suggest a tax, indicating for instance
the advantages of a tax over licensing as a means of
discouraging the sale of certain goods on the domestic
market. Also, possibly at the direction of their superiors,
officials may be set to work examining the economic
implications and revenue possibilities of various alter-
native tax schemes. In these ways officials may make
suggestions and offer advice, but the final selection from

the various possibilities is made only by the most senior officials of the Treasury, by whom it is submitted, as a recommendation, to the Chancellor. The result is that many officials will have a good notion of some part of the Budget, but none, except the Chancellor's immediate advisers, will be informed of the whole. The Chancellor may also, of course, consult with certain ministerial colleagues. And indeed, even members of the public may have a fair assurance of some particular item. For example, Sir Stafford Cripps in his Budget Speech in 1950 observed that the brewers had agreed to increase the gravities of all beers on the understanding that he would so adjust taxation as to avoid additional duty.[1]

With the assistance of his colleagues and officials, and in the light of the decisions made in the previous phases of the planning process—which have themselves been affected by the probable shape of the Budget—the Chancellor in the mid-winter of each year makes his decisions on both expenditure and revenue. Revenue, as we have seen, is his exclusive province. Expenditure, if it must be adjusted, may raise a Cabinet question, as may also any modifications of economic policy. While the Chancellor cannot finally decide such questions, he can and indeed is compelled by his position to insist that they be given a deliberate answer by the Cabinet, and as the minister with the ancient duty of finding the money to cover expenditure as well as the newer task of co-

[1] 474 H.C. Deb. 71 (18 April 1950).

ordinating economic policy he leads from a strong hand.

The system of decisions produced by this process of planning lays down the main lines of economic and financial policy for the year. Yet as a look at any of the recent *Economic Surveys* or Budget Speeches will suggest, these decisions cannot be regarded as fixing without likelihood of change the lines of action for the following twelve months. Immediately after the war, as the *Survey* for 1947 indicates, the belief was widely held that economic planning could be carried out by means of a series of fixed programmes dictating action throughout the year.[1] Along with the decline of faith in quantitative planning, this belief also has withered away. In practice, a continual adjustment of policy goes on between the periods of annual review. Forecasts of the probable course of the economy are periodically prepared in the Treasury. So informed, officials and ministers can have well in advance some idea of the nature and size of the problems they will face when the more elaborate review of events and policy takes place at the end of the year, and will use this knowledge to assess

[1] 'The essence of planning and control by the State in relation to productive industry and commercial activity must be the same in war and peace. I think the essential elements are plans consisting of decisions of policy quantitatively expressed in the form of programmes and such measures as in particular circumstances may be necessary to ensure the performance of these programmes.' Franks, *Central Planning and Control in War and Peace*, p. 17. See also *Economic Survey for 1947*, pp. 4–9.

proposals newly brought forward by officials or ministers. The projects that form the substance of policy are constantly being generated in departmental offices, ministers' heads, and perhaps also parliamentary debates, and brought to the attention of the Treasury, interdepartmental committees, and the Cabinet. To refuse or to deny them permission to proceed to the stage where commitments are made can have a substantial effect on the economy. The 'lead time' involved will, of course, prevent anything that might be called the swift manipulation of the economy. Yet this sort of control makes it possible to begin action to meet a problem without waiting for the yearly review and permits some flexibility in government efforts to influence the economy in the interim between reviews. Indeed, as the main outlines of the estimates of expenditure will have been in large part drawn during the process of day-to-day control by the Supply divisions, so also the basic decisions on economic policy will have been developing during the months preceding the main phases of the planning process.

Who makes these adjustments? Below the Cabinet level what unit, if any, watches over and co-ordinates throughout the year the whole spectrum of economic policy? To reply 'The Treasury' burkes the question because the Treasury is an agency of several hundred administrators and one might well ask, 'Who co-ordinates the Treasury?' The CEPS can claim the role of continually keeping an eye on economic affairs as a whole. It operates, however, as a staff providing assistance to bodies which make official decisions, rather than as a body itself exercising powers of co-ordination. Although it does not perform the ambitious tasks assigned to it in the *Economic Survey* of 1947, the official committee of heads of the economic departments continues to do useful and in a sense indispensable work by providing a forum where the views of the main economic departments can be presented and pulled together and an effort made to get the maximum agreement on policy and problems at the official level. It cannot, however, deal with much of the business involved in the final framing of the Budget. But neither does that business, although it is concerned with much more than the raising of revenue, have as wide a scope as that of the official committee.

To look for formal machinery that will adequately answer the question of who co-ordinates the co-ordinators is to look in vain. As an official in denying there is such a centre may say, 'A responsible civil servant must use his head'. If officials do 'use their heads', that can mean that co-ordination at the highest level is successful only because of certain other conditions as well. During the war, as D. N. Chester has pointed out, there was, in spite of the immense size of the Government and its problems, a quite small group of men in Whitehall, including both ministers and officials, and numbering, he suggests, between twenty and fifty, who held the major threads of government. Living in frequent, almost continual, contact, they were constantly exchanging views and information and it was in this interchange that the real work of overall co-ordination was accomplished.[1] In peacetime also much the same is true. No formal arrangement of committees or staffs could quite free British government of its dependence for co-ordination upon the common-rooms and lunch tables of the clubs of Pall Mall, nor would any unifying set of directives take the place of the strong corporate life of the higher civil service.

[1] *Lessons of the British War Economy* (Cambridge, 1951), D. N. Chester (ed.), pp. 23–24.

IV

THE NATURE OF
THE TREASURY'S POWER

POWER we may take to be the ability of someone to get his decisions accepted by others. Treasury control is a kind of power, but what kind? Is it a power to command, the ability to tell others what they may or may not do? Or is it something less precise, a power of influence, not involving orders or commands, but in the end achieving the same result? What is its content—the ability positively to direct, or merely to negate?[1] On what real, and not simply legal or formal, foundation does it rest in the British administrative system and constitution?

Does the Treasury have the power of command? The contrast between Treasury control and the powers of an 'Economic General Staff' or an agency of joint staff planning indicates that the answer cannot be an unqualified yes. The Treasury's operations are so little in this style that it might seem plausible to say that its

[1] For discussion of these questions, see S. E. Finer, *A Primer of Public Administration*, pp. 53–65, and H. R. G. Greaves, *The Civil Service in the Changing State*, pp. 150 ('The Treasury Dilemma') and 156 ('The need to "Interfere"'). A demand for stronger control and for 'supradepartmental co-ordination' by the Treasury was voiced by the Committee on National Expenditure during the war. See *14th Report, Select Comm. on National Expenditure, 1942–43*, par. 14.

business is not 'direction' but merely the elimination of inconsistencies and overlapping. Yet in trimming expenditure or shaping estimates of investment, surely it does more than this. As we have seen throughout this study, Treasury control, old or new, applies Government policy in deciding what departments may do.

One difference lies in the distinction between 'may' and 'shall'. Of the proposals that departments bring to the Treasury, it says which may or may not be carried out, but by and large the initiative lies with departments and it is not the Treasury's part to tell them positively what they shall do. Indeed, departmental complaints against the Treasury familiarly echo this fact: Treasury control is negative, it is concerned with turning things down. Periodically, we find Treasury spokesmen assuring the world that this is no longer the case and that the Treasury has entered a new and positive phase. Quite possibly Treasury attitudes are more constructive today than they were a generation or two ago. The Treasury will often offer departments advice on how to carry out their proposals and not confine itself simply to saying yes or no. A deliberate effort has been made to encourage Treasury officials to sit in with department officials as partners, not simply critics, at the early stages of discussion of new schemes. Given the nature of some of the economic problems dealt with, this would seem to be unavoidable. Suppose—during the period of bulk purchasing—the Ministry of Food proposed to buy the whole of the West African cocoa crop. Treasury officials would actively discuss with the Ministry other possible sources of supply, times of purchase, and so on. It could hardly make a decision on the request for approval without taking a hold on the substantive problem itself. And certainly the knowledge of Supply officials, gained through service in other departments and experience in dealing with problems of several related departments, would be of real assistance.

An even greater step towards positive direction might be taken if depression were to hit the economy. Then it could quite possibly follow from the 'inflationary-deflationary scheme' that the Treasury would ask for greater expenditure of certain general kinds. Would the Treasury also go so far as to ask departments to undertake particular projects—for instance, the building of a number of ships of specified kinds in order to relieve unemployment in certain yards? And would departments relish a Treasury control so positive that it took the initiative in telling them what they should do? At any rate, the situation has not yet arisen. The positive aid afforded departments remains subordinate to the main business of the Treasury. Although the positive State has arrived, Treasury control remains essentially negative. It must, if the initiative is to remain with departments.

If the Treasury's power is not that of positive direction, is it then at least the power of negative command? The power of prior approval, for instance, is the power by command to negative a proposed departmental activity. Similar was the power to decide what projects should be excluded from the investment programme. It is by means of such powers that the Treasury is able to enforce Government policy.

Yet, as we have seen, 'enforce', even if limited to negative commands, is too strong a word when we consider what actually goes on in the relations of the Treasury and departments. Any Treasury decision at the official level is at the mercy of ministerial reversal. If the departmental official disagrees, he may say he will take up the matter with his minister, who, whether or not of Cabinet rank, has the right, in no way exceptional, of bringing a matter relating to this department before the Cabinet. If the minister has set his heart on a scheme toward which Treasury officials are hostile, the way is open to him to appeal to the Cabinet and possibly win its approval. Similarly, in the United States an agency head dissatisfied with a ruling of the Bureau of the Budget may appeal to the chief executive, the President. But in Britain the more important ministers—that is, the members of the Cabinet—have a position of power quite different from that of the head of an American agency. For the Cabinet minister is not only a department head, he is also part of the chief executive. When the Treasury in the name of the chief executive rules against his department, it is, if the matter is looked at on the ministerial plane, ruling against a part of the chief executive itself. So far therefore as Cabinet ministers' interests are engaged in schemes, how is it possible for the Treasury to have even a power of negative command? The Treasury is only the department of another Cabinet minister, the Chancellor of the Exchequer.

Yet it is perfectly clear that the Treasury does have power. Treasury control, old and new, is an effective system of co-ordination in the service of Government policy. Its formal powers do not, as is the case in some administrative systems, unfaithfully reflect its real powers. In relations with departments it does by and large get its way in decision-making. Yet it is also true that it does not do so by command or direction: departmental officials are not its military subordinates. Shall we say then that the Treasury's power is not the power of command, but the power of influence? The distinction is not merely verbal, but directs attention to real operational traits of Treasury-departmental relations. Supporting the formal powers of the official Treasury is a structure of influence which largely antedates those powers and which has more effect than they upon what goes on in the processes of Treasury control. It rests partly upon the nature of the Civil Service and partly on the nature of the constitution.

Our problem might be stated as this: How is it possible to have an energetic enforcement of policy or even substantial co-ordination under a plural executive? Hamilton's incisive arguments in the 69th *Federalist* (Unity of the Executive Desirable) come to mind: There will be disagreement within the executive council; perhaps factions will form. Decisions will be delayed and, when and if they are made, will be heavy with compromise and lack the unifying rationale of a single mind. It follows, therefore, that if we want energy, direction, co-ordination in the administrative machine and in policy, there must be a single undisputed head of the executive branch. Examples of Cabinet behaviour in other countries with parliamentary government tend strongly to confirm these arguments from common sense. So far as they are sound, it follows that the delay and distraction of a plural executive at the ministerial level will be reflected in the behaviour of the bureaucracy, impeding agreement at that level and impairing the authority of administrative co-ordinators. What factors in the British system tend to offset these possibilities?

Professional standards of the Civil Service

To begin with, there is in British government at the official level a strong tendency to reach agreement and, where conflicts occur, to find as quickly as possible a generally accepted resolution. 'The business of H.M. Government is to govern', 'the law that H.M. Government must be carried on'—to the official, especially of the Administrative Class, these familiar phrases state what the career service is there to do. As a member of this service, the civil servant's function is not to win departmental battles or individual renown, but 'to get on with the job'. Judged by this standard it is not success but failure for officials, when their inability to agree obliges them to refer a question to ministers for decision.

This standard is one of a set that are more or less closely linked and mutually supporting. Another, for instance, is the obligation not to become emotionally committed to the programmes being administered. Common to the profession of bureaucrat in general, although not equally fulfilled in all systems, this obligation is one way in which the bureaucrat differs from the politician.[1] In Britain it results in what some call the 'stoical realism',[2] some the 'cynicism', of the civil servant. It means that he will be able faithfully to serve different Governments and also that he will have remained free of the impediments to agreement which commitment involves.

Simply as such, as professional standards, the force of these conventions should not be underestimated. The Civil Service, in one official's words, is 'an adoptive institution'. It has a certain autonomous corporate life of its own which shapes the new recruit and to which he must adapt himself. In general the similarities are marked with those other forms of corporate social exis-

[1] See Max Weber's famous essay 'Politics as a Vocation', in *From Max Weber: essays in sociology*. Translated and edited with an introduction by H. H. Gerth and C. Wright Mills (New York, 1946).
[2] The phrase is H. E. Dale's. See his *Higher Civil Service of Great Britain*.

113

tence which flourish widely in England and the origins of which often antedate the era of individualism. There is, for instance, more than a hint of the life of the Oxford and Cambridge colleges where many of the members of the higher civil service have been educated. The professional standards of 'reasonableness' and of 'getting on with the job' are backed by the informal sanctions of this corporate life, in particular the approval and disapproval of lifetime colleagues.

None of this may be taken to mean that civil servants are not personally ambitious or competitive. On the contrary, promotion and reputation are eagerly sought and the spirit of the system is not mellow or easy-going. Judgements by equals of one another, as well as by superiors of their subordinates, and, of course, by subordinates of superiors, are rarely softened by sentiment. At each stage of promotion only a few of those who aspire can be chosen and many are the Principals who, after their first period of trial, find themselves relegated to lifetime tasks of routine. To escape such a fate, to rise and become known—within the circle that counts—the individual will strongly exert himself. But his efforts, if they are not to be self-defeating, must be subordinated to the standards of the profession.

The psychology of the British civil servant raises large questions. His professional standards, his feeling for corporate life, his 'due sense of subordination', to use Dale's phrase, can hardly be understood apart from the psychology, not merely of the civil servant, but also of the Englishman and Briton. They need to be stressed here because they are so greatly emphasized by officials themselves. Indeed, to the occasional irritation of the foreign observer, the norms they involve come close to being treated as self-evident principles of morality and, therefore, in need of no further explanation.

Yet we need to point out the support these standards receive from other sources. We can readily conceive, for instance, how the tendency to agree would be disrupted by a system of legislative committees with access to officials and with an effective voice in policy. If officials were regularly called before legislative committees like the American and asked to explain or justify department or Government policy, the administrative process would hardly remain unchanged. This procedure would put in the way of officials the temptation to make an appeal for parliamentary support of their views which perhaps even the 'stoical realism' of the civil servant could not resist. And even if they acted in the best faith, they could hardly fail at times to state and advocate views differing from what would ultimately have been settled on as Cabinet policy. As it is, however, the Civil Service is shut in on itself with ministers as the only outlet of its views into the political world. With no important exceptions, ministers cannot, under the constitution, delegate authority to officials. True, an official may and often does act without consulting his minister. But for whatever his officials do, the minister is responsible to Parliament and about their discretionary actions only he can be questioned. To this rule the questioning of Accounting Officers by the Public Accounts Committee is no exception, as they are called to answer questions touching not the exercise of any discretionary authority but the legality of their actions under the rules regulating financial procedure, and although the inquiry will also branch out into questions of efficiency, it cannot deal with policy.

Ministerial responsibility assures the Government's control over the administration and at the same time protects the administration from having to answer to two masters. An extension of the powers of parliamentary committees might well jeopardize these consequences and the principle upon which they rest. In 1946 the Select Committee on Procedure considered a proposal that there be set up a Committee on Public Expenditure, combining the functions of the Estimates and the Public Accounts Committees, possessing wide powers to question civil servants and assisted by 'a sufficient body of trained clerks'. Remarking that the term 'trained clerk' had caused 'certain reverberations in Whitehall', Mr. Herbert Morrison, then Lord President of the Council, took strong exception to this proposal on the ground that it might impair ministerial responsibility. 'Parliament's business', he said, 'is to check the Government, throw it out if it wants to, go for it, attack it, criticise it, by all means, but Parliament is not a body which is organised for current administration—not in this country. They have had a go at it in France and the United States, and I do not think too much of it.'[1]

Effect of plural executive

In particular, the situation in which the British plural executive puts the official strongly supports the tendency toward agreement and for precisely the same reason that makes Treasury 'direction' impossible. The Cabinet minister is not only head of a department; he is also a part of the executive organ which is responsible for making Government policy as a whole and which will have to resolve any conflicts that officials cannot settle. It follows that the official, while obliged in his dealings with other departments to represent his minister's view, is not impelled to be as self-assertive as he would be if his minister were simply the head of a department and responsible only for its success. The minister has his view of what the department ought to do. But if the Cabinet overrules him—unless he chooses to resign— he will have to accept that decision. And the Cabinet's decision will be the minister's decision, not only in the sense that he will be obliged to carry it out and publicly defend it, not only in the sense that he will have taken part in the deliberations from which it emerged, but also in the sense that he will have been an indispensable part

[1] 3rd Report, *Select Committee on Procedure 1946*; Minutes of Evidence, p. 111.

of the body that deliberated and decided. Formally and psychologically the decision will be his to an extent it could not be if he were overruled in whole or in part by another person possessing the whole executive power. (The situation is different for the minister who is not a member of the Cabinet, but we are speaking here of the score or so of principal ministers who are members.) In the face of this possibility, the official, even if he is thinking only of faithfully representing his minister, will be to some extent restrained in asserting the departmental view. If his minister were only a departmental head, there would be a certain disloyalty in qualifying his championship of the department's view in anticipation of defeat at the hands of the chief executive. But when the minister is himself a part of the chief executive, it can hardly be disloyal to anticipate what he would say and—more or less—think, if the chief executive were called upon to decide. In general, and of course with many exceptions in practice, the effect of this situation is that discussions at the official level tend to reflect the probabilities of decision at the ministerial level and, as compared with the situation under a unitary executive, the tendency to agreement is enhanced.

This dependence of the course of business at the official level upon its course at the ministerial level is revealed by those exceptional times when the Cabinet cannot reach agreement. Such a period was the latter part of World War II when, anticipating that victory would soon break up the Coalition, its members began to foresee their party differences over the coming issues of peace-time and found it hard to reach agreement on matters not immediately connected with the war. This difficulty of decision at the ministerial level impeded the work of officials in making plans for reconstruction and other post-war programmes. A similar impediment may also be created by the differences of strong-minded ministers within a Government based on a single party.

The tendency to agreement proceeding from the professional standards of the Civil Service and from the structure of Britain's executive power does not, of course, by itself suffice to account for the power of the Treasury. It is compatible with a situation in which official decisions result from a balance of pressures on which the Treasury has exerted no more force than any other department. Conceivably, agreement could be quickly and regularly reached by a process of compromise which, while satisfying the claimants in relation to one another, showed insufficient regard for the needs of general economic and financial policy. Something of the sort happened before the reforms of 1947. And throughout, this study has tried not to exaggerate the degree of rationality reached by Treasury control. Departmental pressures flowing partly from administrative and partly from political sources may strain the best efforts of co-ordinators.

Administrative machinery has a bearing on the

problem. Interdepartmental committees are indispensable, but it is quite possible that in recent years their proliferation has gone too far, blurring the responsibility of departments and individuals and preventing proposals from reaching ministers until after they have been 'chewed over, regurgitated and generally reduced to a bland, possibly nutritive, but entirely tasteless chyle'. Some officials will even at times express a certain wistful admiration for the more loose-knit American system where, as they say, the daring and original idea, although there is no guarantee it will survive in the final operative decisions, at least has the chance to reach the public.[1]

Whatever the responsibility of administrative machinery may be, it remains that government decisions in Britain will often be heavy with compromise. In American government the process of compromise is carried out largely in public—with much wear and tear on the

[1] 'By the time the civil service has finished drafting a document to give effect to a principle', Lord Reith has written, 'there may be little of the principle left.' J. C. W. Reith, *Into the Wind* (London, 1949). D. N. Chester has summed up more judiciously: 'The great value of the Whitehall process with its numerous interdepartmental committees and its stress on clearing matters at all levels with interested departments is that any course of action finally agreed upon is usually practicable, at least it is practicable in the eyes of Whitehall. Included in the term practicable is the acceptance of the policy by all the departments who will have some part in its administration. The danger inherent in the process, indeed in any process in which a large number of interests and considerations have to be taken into account, is that the ideal course of action may be completely lost sight of in the discussion of departmental difficulties and objections.' *Lessons of the British War Economy*, D. N. Chester (ed.), p. 14.

nerves and some addition to the gaiety of existence. In Britain it is carried on behind scenes. The pressures there composed are on the whole less divisive and stubborn and the structure of government is less prone than the American to exacerbating and 'institutionaliz-ing' conflict. Compromise, however, continually goes on and Treasury control is one of its main channels. From this it follows that Treasury control cannot be expected to do too much. It is not suited to planning on the military model. It cannot be expected to direct and co-ordinate policy that depends for its success upon the exact fulfilment of quantitative programmes precisely fitted together in advance by the planner's mind or the calculating machine. In the decisions that flow from it there will be too much of the administrator's judgement and of committee compromise.

Treasury control can, however, deal with the kind of economic planning in which 'by and large' suggests the degree of exactness aimed at and in which the parts are not so tightly knit together but what considerable errors here and there are tolerable and frequent adjustment is feasible. The Keynesian categories are admirably suited to its powers. The British political system with its disci-plined majorities would seem to be much better able than most to tolerate wide public acceptance of the Keynesian promise of full employment without plunging into run-away inflation. So also the British administra-tive system is peculiarly fitted to carry out the duty of

WORKING MEN'S
COLLEGE
LIBRARY

co-ordination entailed by this promise and the economic analysis on which it is founded.

Authority of the Chancellor of the Exchequer

As is necessary under the present variety of planning, Treasury control is, however, more than a channel of compromise. For in reflecting the probabilities of ministerial decision, discussion among officials lends great influence to the Treasury view. Ministers, even those in the Cabinet, are not by any means all equal. The Prime Minister, for instance, while not the chief executive, is, as the phrase goes, 'first among equals'. What this phrase means in decision-making by the Cabinet will vary with many factors. In most Governments it will mean that he can without great difficulty overrule or even drop from office almost any minister except those few constituting the 'inner Cabinet'.

Similarly, in relation to other ministers, the Chancellor of the Exchequer usually has a pre-eminent position. He will be almost invariably a member of the inner Cabinet and often the heir apparent to the leader of the party. Apart from the party and political prestige he may enjoy, he, like the Prime Minister, gains in authority from the special responsibility of his office. As the framing of the Budget shows, he has the traditional duty of finding the money to meet government expenditure. Although the Cabinet can overrule him, as it can any other minister, this duty is central to his individual ministerial responsibility. But this responsibility implies a kind of authority in relation to the activities of other departments that is unique. In time of war the Minister of Labour in charge of manpower may have a like position of power. But in peace-time and under the present kind of economic planning, upon the minister who is responsible to Parliament for proposing how the money is to be raised to finance the Government's programmes, departments are peculiarly dependent. He does not merely advise the chief executive on the methods of finance which the legislature will be requested to adopt. It is his individual responsibility to decide what methods are to be proposed to Parliament, subject only to the Cabinet's power to overrule him in the extreme case. It follows that he will have a voice in the control of expenditure. 'If he is to be held responsible for filling the reservoir and maintaining a certain depth of water in it,' as the Haldane Committee said, 'he must also be in a position to regulate the outflow.'[1] Since

[1] Cmd. 9230. *Report of the Machinery of Government Committee* (1918), p. 18. Of the Chancellor of the Exchequer, Mr. Gladstone said: 'Though he has no right to demand the concurrence of his colleagues in his view of the estimates, he has a rather special right, because these do so much towards determining budget and taxation, to indicate his own views by resignation' (Quoted in Jennings, *Cabinet Government* (2nd edn.), p. 149). '. . . the praise and political power which an elected body gets from spending money on social and other services', writes D. N. Chester, 'has to be measured against the direct political harm which the elected body may suffer when taxes corresponding to the expenditure have to be levied. Here, of course, is the source of the Chancellor of the Exchequer's power.

policy depends to a very great extent upon expenditure, this means that he has a power, unique among the powers of all ministers except the Prime Minister, to influence the policy of departments. This unique power is reflected in deliberations at the official level, strengthening the hand of Treasury officials. It means that the tendency to agreement produces not simply compromise but decisions shaped around the Treasury view.

'Treasury control has no basis save the authority in the Cabinet of the Chancellor of the Exchequer',[1] and that authority, so far as it is derived from his office, rests upon his responsibility for revenue proposals and such further power over proposed expenditure as this responsibility implies. Yet this does not seem to be quite the end of the analysis, if we are looking for the real bases of his power. Does not his authority over expenditure include some direct, as well as implied, control over expenditure and, in the realities of the situation, does not his department, as well as his position in the Cabinet, have powers which in turn strengthen him?

Treasury control, as we have seen, antedates the financial reforms of the Gladstonian era. These reforms did much to centralize and improve financial administration, but they were in harmony with the design of the

No Chancellor would accept responsibility for his taxes had he not, in consequence, the special position in respect of all Government policy involving expenditure.' *Central and Local Government* (London, 1951), p. 31.

[1] Jennings, *Cabinet Government*, 2nd edn., p. 150.

ancient monarchic edifice. At one time Britain had in fact a unitary executive. Parliament made grants to His or Her Majesty who in turn used the Treasury, which then meant a Lord High Treasurer or a Board, as the traditional instrument for issuing funds to defray the costs of government. The records show, for instance, William III discussing with his Treasury Lords not only financial questions but also matters with a strangely contemporary ring, such as the balance of trade with the colonies and establishments questions such as the number of persons employed in a government office and the fees they received.[1] The Sovereign addressed to the Treasury his orders for the issue of money for various purposes and all issues had to be supported by Treasury warrant. From the Restoration until the time of George II, it is said that the Treasury exercised a more detailed control over expenditure than it has in modern times; to its meetings, held several times a week, it summoned applicants to whom it gave direct orders. Then, writes Heath, 'every department lived from hand to mouth looking to the Treasury for its daily bread'.[2]

The historical origins of a power do not necessarily reveal the foundations on which it rests today. A long-continued practice, however, may have, quite apart from

[1] For an account of a primitive 'O & M' inquiry see the paper entitled 'Hearing before the King about Mismanagement in the Excise', *Calendar of Treasury Papers*: edited by Joseph Redington, vol. ii (London, 1871), Preface, p. xxiii.

[2] *The Treasury*, p. 11.

other factors, an influence simply as such, as a traditional practice. Simply being ancient, particularly in Britain, can be important. What this reference to the practice of Treasury control in the days of real monarchic governments suggests is that the Treasury's power enjoys such support, its authority resting in part upon traditional practices considerably antedating the rise of Cabinet Government and of the individual ministerial responsibility of the Chancellor of the Exchequer for revenue proposals. This is also the common sense of the matter. The sentiments underlying the attitude of Treasury and departmental officials—'The Treasury's the Treasury. Who else should control expenditure?'—cannot be reduced to merely a reflection of the Chancellor's implied powers over expenditure. Tradition endows not only the Chancellor but also the Treasury, as an institution including both officials and ministers, with a certain authority. It follows that if the Chancellor has power in the Cabinet, it is in part because he heads a powerful department.

An historical approach also suggests another question. Today, as in the past, Parliament in law still makes its grants not to departments but to Her Majesty, who has previously requested them through one of her ministers. It follows that the expenditure of appropriations is not mandatory. 'Money', as Maitland put it, 'is granted to the queen; it is placed at the disposal of her and her ministers. But she and they are not bound by law to spend it, at least not bound by the Appropriations Act.'[1] The question from time to time controverted in the United States, viz. whether the Executive is obliged to spend money simply *because* it has been appropriated,[2] could not arise in Britain. If the Cabinet chooses to

---

[1] F. W. Maitland, *Constitutional History of England* (Cambridge, 1908), pp. 445–6.

[2] The President has the power, clarified by the General Appropriation Act of 1950, to require departments to hold appropriated funds in reserve when he deems expenditure of such funds not to be needed. The justification for such action, however, according to the Act, is 'to provide for contingencies, or to effect savings whenever savings are made possible by or through changes in requirements, greater efficiency of operations or other developments' (see Smithies, *Budgetary Process*, pp. 149–50). This is quite a different matter from the President's ordering a department not to spend certain funds because he disapproves of the programme covered by the appropriation. 'I would not object', said one Congressman, '. . . to any reasonable economies in Government. But economy is one thing and the abandonment of a policy and program of the Congress another thing' (Elias Huzar, *The Purse and the Sword: Control of the Army by Congress through Military Appropriations, 1933–1950* (Ithaca, 1950), p. 364).

Whether appropriations are in this sense mandatory has occasionally given rise to conflicts between the President and Congress. In 1949, for example, President Truman ordered that the National Military Establishment should spend funds for only the forty-eight air groups he had recommended in his budget for 1949–50 instead of the fifty-eight groups for which Congress had appropriated money. Later at hearings before a House appropriations sub-committee, this action was attacked, critics arguing that since 'the Congress under the Constitution decides how much money is to be expended for the services and is charged with the responsibility of raising and maintaining the armed forces, . . . anything done contrary to this is . . . contrary to the basic law of the land.' For a discussion of this question, see Huzar, pp. 362 ff.

spend less than the sum appropriated for—say—the Air Force and to use the Treasury to carry out this decision, neither the Air Minister nor his department nor Parliament could raise a constitutional or legal objection.

From this fact of financial procedure it follows that there must be some further step beyond appropriation before departments may proceed to the expenditure of funds. Such parliamentary authorization as they have is necessary, but not sufficient. The money having been granted to Her Majesty, she must indicate her desire that it be spent. This is done when Her Majesty by royal order under the Royal Sign Manual countersigned by the Treasury authorizes and requires the Treasury to issue sums required to defray the expenses specified in the Appropriation Acts. The Treasury in turn orders issues from its credits on the Exchequer Account at the Bank of England to the Paymaster General, on whom departments draw for the sums they require.

This procedure developed from ancient legal formalities which once expressed the reality of royal control of expenditure. But could present-day Treasury control have arisen if these formalities had not existed? Under them, once grants have been made to the Crown, the Treasury controls their expenditure. This being so, it is a short step to giving the Treasury the power to ensure beforehand that departmental activities are such that the Crown shall be ready to spend money on them once funds are available. In this sense the requirement of prior approval merely anticipates the Crown's and the Treasury's power under these ancient formalities directly to control expenditure. And when that requirement has been established, the formalities of the Crown's control seem to become mere formalities. But are they?

It is a teasing question and one of a sort that frequently arises in the study of British government. With Bagehot we distinguish between the 'dignified' and 'efficient' parts of the constitution and learn how the formalities of the former have very largely been reduced to mere formalities. Yet again and again the question arises whether an 'efficient' part would work if the formalities were removed. If the formalities of royal control were removed, how much effect would remain to the power of requiring prior approval? Suppose appropriations were to be made not to the Crown but directly to departments. Would this not change the whole atmosphere of the system? It is hard to believe that the power of requiring prior approval would not be gravely impaired.

Yet even if this speculation be granted, does it follow that the formalities of royal control add to the Chancellor's real power in the Cabinet? Nowadays the legal powers of the Crown are exercised by the Cabinet. How, therefore, can the Chancellor gain from them additional power in his relations with other ministers? Certainly the Chancellor would not attempt to exercise these formal powers against the Cabinet's will. But that is not the question. The real question here is not what might conceivably happen, but what the existing set of factors tends to cause to happen. Suppose some difference of opinion over proposed expenditure arises between the Chancellor and another Cabinet minister. Both are members of the body which must resolve the disagreement. The minister also speaks with the authority of the person responsible for his department's policy. But he confronts in the Chancellor not only the minister responsible for revenue proposals but also the head of the department which by ancient formality and actual daily practice controls expenditure, present and prospective. To the power of the Chancellor's office and to his weight in Cabinet deliberations, this must add some imponderable element of authority. He and his department have powers that are mutually strengthening.

As we might expect, there proves to be no single factor which we can isolate and identify as the source of the Treasury's power. Administrative machinery has its importance. So also have the Gladstonian financial reforms and the case law of Treasury control of expenditure, reinforced by the professional standards and conditions of service of the unified Civil Service. Not least important are the effects of the structure of the plural executive, shaped in distinctive ways by Britain's monarchic past. From the thrust and counter-thrust of forces which build up from many sources, the architec-

ture of British government produces the balanced power
of the Treasury and its style of co-ordination.

NOTE ON SOURCES

Among older books which are still useful are A. J. V. Durrell's
Parliamentary Grants (1917) and W. F. Willoughby's *Finan-
cial System of Great Britain* (1917). Other sources of infor-
mation on the Treasury are: R. G. Hawtrey, *The Exchequer
and the Control of Expenditure* (London, 1921); Sir Thomas
Heath, *The Treasury* (London, 1927); H. R. G. Greaves, *The
Civil Service in the Changing State* (London, 1947); S. E.
Finer, *A Primer of Public Administration* (London, 1950);
Sir W. Ivor Jennings, *Cabinet Government*, 2nd edn. (Cam-
bridge, Eng., 1951); Sir Edward Bridges's Stamp Memorial
Lecture, *Treasury Control* (London, 1950); Sir John Woods,
'Treasury Control', *Political Quarterly*, Oct.–Dec. 1954;
D. N. Chester, 'Machinery of Government and Planning' in
The British Economy 1945–1950, G. D. N. Worswick and
P. H. Ady (eds.) (Oxford, 1952), where references to dis-
cussions of the methods and machinery of economic plan-
ning will be found.

INDEX

Accounting Officers, 62, 116; of Establishments divisions, 60; of Supply divisions, 59–60.

Administrative Class of civil servants, 5, 59, 76, 112.

administrative machinery, 119–21, 130.

Admiralty, the, 84.

Ady, P. H., 72 n. 2, 131.

aeroplanes, 50.

agriculture, 29.

American aid, 9, 32; annual review of estimates, 33–35; Appropriation Acts, 40, 43–44, 50, 127 n. 2; appropriations committees, 39–40; authorizations, 50; Budget Bureau, *see* Budget Bureau; budgeting, 25, 38–39; Civil Service Commission, 10; Comptroller General, 60–61; Defense Department, 39; investigating committee, 63; loan, 71.

Anderson, Sir J., 68 n. 1, 69 n. 1, 70.

Anne, Queen, 4.

annual review of estimates, 32–36, 57, 77; American procedure, 33, 35.

appropriation accounts: annual audit, 60–62.

Appropriation Acts, 40–43, 50–52, 60, 127–8; American, 40, 43–44, 50, 127 n. 2.

appropriations: British and American, 45–56, 127–8.

Auditor General, *see* Comptroller.

audits, annual, 48.

Austria: Control Commission in, 63.

authority of the Chancellor of the Exchequer, 122–31.

Bagehot, Walter, 129.

balance of payments, 9, 67, 71, 75, 85, 89, 98.

balance of trade, 125.

Bank of England, 7–8, 128.

Bank of Ireland, 7.

B.B.C., 63.

Bevan, Aneurin, 30–31.

Beveridge, Lord, 68 n. 1.

Board of Customs and Excise, 7.

Board of Inland Revenue, 7.

Board of Trade, 34, 70–71, 82.

borrowing and taxation, 14.

Bridges, Sir Edward, 1 n. 1, 15 n. 1, 64, 66, 131.

British administration, co-ordination in, 4; Civil Service, 4 (*see also* Civil Service); Civil Service Commission, 10; constitution, 4.

Budget: budgetary process, 3, 38–40; and economic planning, 87–88, 93–94, 98–99; final shape of, 98; framing the budget, 7, 25, 66, 83, 99–106; Speech, 39–40; surplus, 93, 97.

budget, American (*see also* Budget Bureau), 25–26, 38.

Budget Bureau, American, 26, 34, 37–38, 58, 110; Estimates division of, 35.

budgets for manpower, &c., 73.

building licences, 84, 87.

Cabinet: fixes government expenditure, 14.

'Cabinet Democracy', 75–76, 78.

Cabinet Ministers: and power of